GET SUPPORT FROM YOUR

ANCESTRY

TO BE WHO YOU ARE

GET SUPPORT FROM YOUR

ANCESTRY

TO BE WHO YOU ARE

ILSE SAND

Translated by Alan Frost

CONTENTS

Let your ancestry give you the courage to be who you are

When I was in my twenties, I only had an uncertain sense of who I was. And I was far more concerned with performance than with experiencing and enjoying life. In unfamiliar social situations, I did not try to sense what I needed or wanted to say or do. My only concern was figuring out what it would take to make the other person like me. And if I had a different opinion to the person I was with, I would not dare to share it. My life has since been a process towards becoming more and more confident about who I am and finding increasingly greater courage to just be – and to express – myself in the world.

How much you know, feel and dare to stand your ground depends to a large extent on your roots. Perhaps your parents or grandparents were able to see you as the person you are, which let them support you in expressing yourself. Or maybe they were unable to see you on your own terms, and you had to try to become the person they saw or adapt to their needs. If the latter is the case, you may have drifted away from yourself and might live with a very fluctuating sense of who you are and what you contain. The good news is that it is never too late. You can still get the support you need to be yourself.

Have you been truly seen?

Feeling seen is a strongly life-affirming experience. It can occur when someone meets you openly and without reservations, without any agenda about what they want to get out of the encounter. You may have experienced – perhaps only briefly – what it is like when the other person answers you on the exact same wavelength that you are transmitting on, and you recognise yourself in her tone or facial expressions. Like when you express joy and her face lights up in a smile, and you see your joy glittering in her eyes. Or when you let sorrow reveal itself in your gaze and see it reflected in the facial expression of the other person. It can also be a comment that makes you feel seen, for example, when a colleague exclaims: "You would probably have liked to make a difference", and you feel that they hit the nail on the head.

As children – or later in life – it is by seeing ourselves reflected in the reaction other people have to us that we discover who we are. If you had people around you who could truly see you, you would therefore have a stable self-understanding.

In this sense, there are no parents who are always able to see their children. Most people manage it in some – perhaps special – cases, while at other times, they mostly see themselves in the children.

Do you have internal support to be yourself?

If you have been seen to a sufficient extent and have received support and recognition, you will – in most contexts – express yourself naturally and without fear whenever you want or find necessary. The kind, affirmative looks and supportive remarks of your relatives – or those of others – have moved into you, so to speak, and have become an internal support. If you have internal support, you can support yourself and stand your ground in situations where everyone around you thinks differently.

However, having or not having support is rarely either-or. You may have internal support to express some aspects of yourself, while feeling fear when you consider expressing others. I would guess that it is easier for you to express yourself when you are happy than, say, when you are feeling envious or helpless. At least that is the case for most people.

Here are some pointers to give you an idea of how much support you have:

Signs of a lack of internal support:

- You feel doubt about yourself and your own worth, for example, when receiving criticism, being rejected or being overlooked.
- You grow uncomfortable when you stand out from the people you are with.
- You feel uncertain if others will be able to like you after you have made a mistake.

- You often refrain from voicing your opinion when it differs to the people around you.
- You often, entirely automatically, suppress certain feelings, for example, when you are sad or angry.
- You hide your positive feelings for someone else if you are not 100% sure that they are reciprocated.
- In certain social situations, your face solidifies into a smile, and you find it hard to let it relax.
- You hide behind a mask, which could be a rapid stream of words, silence or loud laughter.
- In the company of others, you are often up on your toes, as if you are struggling to earn the right to join the community.
- You express yourself as the person you have decided to be, rather than feeling inward and expressing what you want or need.

If you recognise yourself in several of the above statements, you could benefit from getting a lot more internal support. Sometimes we do not know what we are missing until the day we get it. And that is when we suddenly realise that this was exactly what we needed in order to feel more whole.

Get support with ancestry therapy

Both through my personal and professional work, I have discovered the healing power of combining a specific way of seeing your relatives with candid and vulnerable communication. I have chosen to call the method ancestry therapy. Naturally, it can be used by professional therapists; however, in this book, the focus is on how you can use the method to heal yourself through your kin. Ancestry therapy can help you experience that you are being seen and that you are receiving loving confirmation from important kinfolk, and it can help you remove painful bruises left from hurtful interactions.

An honest and direct approach

The method consists of two parts. One part is communication, which could be done, for example, by using letters. As a rule, these should not be sent, but only written for your own sake. Thus, you can work with the method without necessarily involving any of your kinfolk. This means that if your relative is deceased or simply unwilling or unable to see you and give you recognition, this will not hinder you in the slightest.

Writing letters to the dead and to those you have lost in other ways is a well-known therapeutic technique. Saying what is left to be said helps in the mourning process. This book can help you determine what you need to say – whether you need to say it to the living or the dead.

Another option, which in my experience works even better, is to write a letter addressed the other way – i.e. from one of your relatives to you. This will not only give you the confirmation you need, but you also get to learn more about your own deeper desires and longings.

You might think that writing to yourself from a relative will feel artificial or staged. But most people find that once they get started, it becomes much easier than they thought. And you will probably be surprised by the profound release that the letters can give you, even if you wrote them yourself.

If you do not like writing, you can replace the letters with other methods, such as a dialogue between folding paper dolls, which you can find at the back of the book. Or you can set up two chairs opposite each other, imagine that you and a relative are sitting across from each other, and let a conversation take place.

Your relative in her essence

In addition to honest communication, as described above, you should imagine that your relative is present in her essence when you communicate with her. In the book, when I talk about a human being's essence, I mean the person's core, unspoiled by the scars of life. When we are present in our essence, the heart is naturally open, and we can feel and express love without fear.

Very young children can easily access their essence, but many of us adults have lost touch with our innermost being and are rarely in contact with ourselves on that level. But suddenly, we may discover that the connection is there, and we are present amid a torrent of vivacity. It can feel like if we have come into contact with a little piece of heaven within ourselves.

On special occasions, such as by a deathbed, the dying person and the relatives around her sometimes feel an unfamiliar closeness, and they can express a love so strong that it even surprises them. In such cases, they have probably come into contact with their essence – spurred by the gravity of the situation.

When you write to yourself from your relative, you should imagine the person as she is in her essence. You might never have met her like that in reality. Perhaps in her everyday life she is more or less fused with her façade or with the roles she plays. Perhaps she has identified herself as being "the skilled one", "the funny one", "the one people pity" or "the one who has things under control". To be present in your essence is to let go of all the adjectives you would like to be associated with and just be – without trying to be anything specific. Instead, be in the present – with honesty and vulnerability.

If you find it difficult to envision it, it might help if you to imagine that your relative has woken up in the middle of the night with a clear-sightedness that she does not normally have. In that state, you let her write a loving letter to you. A letter in which she says what you have been wanting to hear and which she may not be able to say in real life. You may be surprised by how strong an effect it can have to receive an apology, for example – even if you wrote it yourself.

The reason why your relationship to your ancestry is so important

Your parents, grandparents and all your kinfolk have had a great influence on you becoming who you are today. Even if they are dead, and even if you have never met them, they are significant. You carry their genes, and perhaps you have some thoughts and inner images about them. Your inner images may be composed of what you have been told, experiences you have had with them or what you imagined when looking at photographs. Recent research in epigenetics also suggests that experiences can be passed down across several generations, which means that the experiences of your ancestor may also have influenced you.

Your relatives are, in one way or another, part of your current self-perception. For this reason, how you perceive their attitude towards you is of great importance, i.e. whether they are critical and want to change you or whether you have their support.
It is easy for us to repeat the behavioural patterns of our parents. And they may be repeating their parents' relational style. A certain way of dealing with those closest to you can be passed down through several generations. We either repeat directly, thus copying them, or we repeat inversely, thus trying to do the opposite. An example of the latter could be the daughter of a dependent mother, who, as an adult, refuses to compromise because she does not want to let others have too much influence on her life. She is pleased that she does not look

like her mother, and she may not realise that her own actions are as inflexible and challenging as her mother's compliance.

It is extremely important for your well-being that you find an emotional peace in your relationship to the people who gave and taught you about life. And that you come to an acceptance of the fact that they are as they are and that you are the way you are. Otherwise, the relationship with them will easily spill into other relationships. For example, you might think that you need to give everything you have to your friends because that was what it took in your childhood home. Or you might be putting pressure on your partner because you fail to realise that what you feel you need from him is really something you should have had from your parents.

Often, we are not aware of how much we repeat or how much this imprint is involved in the challenges we face today. You may find that when you start working on your relationship to your ancestor, there are problems in other relationships that dissipate or that you suddenly understand much better.

Pain and joy are passed down through generations

Perhaps you live with a pain caused by not being given what you need by one of your parents. The pain could, for example, lead to anger towards your mother, and it may block your desire to be close to her or your ability to feel compassion for her.
A broader perspective can make a difference. Your mother's ability to give you what you need depends, in part, on what she

herself received from her parents. And, in turn, what they were able to give her depends in part on their parents. Among kin, pain and joy are passed on from one generation to another.

Imagine that behind your mother stands your grandmother, and behind her your great-grandmother and your great-great-grandmother, etc. You can also imagine that your grandfather stands behind your mother, with his father behind him, etc. So there are two rows of relatives behind your mother, and they are constantly branching out.

Sometimes, I suggest to a client that she should direct the anger she feels about her childhood to her entire ancestry, instead of, for example, directing it solely at her father. This can unburden the relationship with her father to the point where something new can begin to happen between them. Sometimes this results in the father being able to provide healing love to his daughter.

Directing your anger towards your whole ancestry, rather than just one person, can be a good intermediary point. The day you are strong enough to contain your own pain and sorrow, your urge to direct your anger outwards and blame your ancestor will dissipate by itself.

The root of your pain stretches back across generations. But you have the opportunity to put an end to a few or a lot of the dysfunctional aspects passed down in your family so that future generations will have fewer inherited burdens to bear. And the good parts that you contribute will also be passed down, link by link, by your descendants.

So, when you work with ancestry therapy, you are not just healing yourself. You are healing your kin.

The natural order

Parents must provide love, care and confirmation to their children, who then pass it on to their children and who, in turn, pass it on to their children. It is the parents' task to accommodate their children's feelings and reactions so that the children learn to be comfortable with what they feel inside and get help to care about themselves.

In some families this is turned on its head, so it is the parents who expect to receive care or joy from their children, and the children are overly concerned with the well-being of the parents. In a way, they take on the parental role relative to their parents. This change of role causes problems, in part because the children will not get what they need to grow strong emotionally. And the role reversal passes on a deficit to future generations since children who have had to act as parents to their parents have less to pass on to their own children.

We should not have expectations of receiving anything from our children, but we should make sure that we get everything possible from our ancestors so that we have something good to pass on.

In families where this functions properly, children are firmly anchored, like a tree that sucks nourishment up through its roots. They gain strength from knowing that they have the support of their kin.

If you do not have children

Several times in the book, I write about passing down something good to our children. For those who do not have children: I hope that every time I refer to *children*, you think of the people you care about and to whom you are giving something. It could be your boyfriend's children, nephews or nieces. Or maybe you are passing things on through art, music or your work, by creating something good or spreading joy. Or perhaps you are the type who always smiles at the clerk, who then goes home and feels energised enough to do something nice for her child – and that way you are leaving an imprint on future generations. We all pass on something, whether we have children or not.

Don't you want contact?

Perhaps you have chosen not to see one or more of your kinfolk anymore. I do not encourage you to resume contact if it is not good for you. For some people, it is best not to have contact with a parent or a grandparent.

Some people do not want to receive anything from one or more of their closest relatives because they are afraid that they will end up resembling them or living their lives. But when you use the tools of ancestry therapy, you can let your relatives give you something positive without adopting their neuroses and their counterproductive behavioural patterns. And this is fortunate because you need their blessing, and through them the blessing of your entire ancestry. And that which you receive, you will then be able to pass on to your children or to whomever you are important to. You should not accept it for your ancestor's sake, but to have something good to pass on.

Choosing to cut contact only solves part of the problem since you are carrying their genes and, in a way, they live inside you. For example, sometimes you just know what your mother would say in a certain situation, without having to ask her first. You therefore pay a price if you live with negative thoughts and feelings in relation to your ancestors. The price may be that you have distanced yourself from that part of you that resembles the relative in question, and you are therefore living with the inner feeling that you are missing something because you have completely or partially lost connection to a part of yourself.

If you use ancestry therapy to reconcile with your relative, you can subsequently experience a new inner peace that lets you breathe deeper and with more freedom – even if you still do not want to see them.

Dialogue between *I* and *you* – a cornerstone of ancestry therapy

When we talk about a relationship pain, it often becomes a story "about" the other person and ourselves. We recount what the other person did or said, how we contributed, and how it affected us. We might have spoken about this relationship multiple times, and now we can do it without getting very emotional and without experiencing either relief or new insights.

If, instead of talking "about", you start addressing the other party in the relationship directly, you will add a new dimension, and something completely new could happen. As a psychotherapist, I often experience this shift. Here is an example:

Irene tells me about her painful relationship with her father. She talks about what her father says and does, and what she wishes he had said and done instead. At one point, I put a chair in front of her and ask her to imagine her father sitting in the chair. Then I ask her to say what she just told me, but directly to him. And now, something new happens. She grows quiet and searches for the words. What Irene is saying is being formulated in this precise moment: Dad, I feel so … or: Dad, you probably never knew that …. The mood becomes intense, and the emotions are strong. Instead of talking "about" her father and focusing on him, Irene now searches inward and speaks from within. When you contact a "you" directly, it always happens in the moment. It is unpredictable and can awaken new thoughts and feelings and a deeper presence.

When you want to express something directly to a "you", you can of course seek out the person in real life if they are still alive. But here it should be about how you can do it without involving the other party.

For example, you could communicate with the other person by talking to a photo, you can talk to a relative by pretending she is sitting in an empty chair in front of you, or you can write a letter. In a book, it is easier to provide examples of the latter, which is why most of the book presents instructions for letter writing with examples. You can transfer the instructions to the other methods, where you just talk rather than write.

No matter which of the tools you choose, the secret behind their power to transform or release is that there is an "I" that addresses a "you". Either you contact a relative directly, or you let a relative approach you directly.

Contents of the book

The first chapters of the book include many examples of letters. Then follow a few chapters that give you very specific advice on how to approach this method when you want to work with it. After that you will find a few chapters on how you can process your letters and how to proceed if the relative in question is still alive and burdening you.

In Chapter Eight, I describe how you can use the alternative tools instead of – or as a variation to – the letters. Chapter Nine is about forgiveness and reconciliation, and Chapter Ten is about how you can improve your ability to contain your emotions and achieve greater freedom.

You can benefit from reading the book even if you do not want to start using the ancestry therapy tools. Just by reading the numerous examples, you will find inspiration to think new thoughts about yourself and your family.

The book is written in easy-to-read language and is relevant to anyone interested in psychology and relationships.

Instead of using "he or she" I have chosen to consistently use "she" in the book when referring to people with unknown genders.

Letters that release you

In the autumn of 2021, I attended a meditation evening in a Buddhist context. Here I overheard the comment: "Many of us have a complicated relationship with our parents." My emotional response was: "I no longer have." At that time, my more loving relationship with my parents was something entirely new. Since then, I have discovered how much it means to have the clear feeling that my parents and grandparents (and through them my entire family) are standing behind me and supporting me.

When my mother was alive, our relationship was complicated. If I was with her for more than two hours, I would be flooded with something resembling a depression. Everything would turn black, and I felt so wrong that I could get the idea that it would be easier for everyone if I were dead.

My mother often said: "Why do you always write about such sad topics? Why don't you write about the joy? No one wants to read something so sad." At that time, I had the condescending thought: "Why don't you write a book about the joy yourself? But you have no self-discipline. It will never happen, and even if it did, your book would be so superficial that no one would read it." I never said it out loud. I only thought it and withdrew into myself.

When I think of my mother today, I mostly feel gratitude. I am grateful for the good experiences we had together, even though they were rare. Because she gave me life, and because she cared deeply that I was doing well.

A few years ago I wrote angry letters to my mother – at the request of a teacher during my education as a psychotherapist. Letters that I never sent. Even though they were written for my own sake, I do not remember them helping. But perhaps they helped pave the way for the letter to my mother, which released me and which you can read a little later.

There was a time when guilt was the strongest feeling I felt in relation to my mother. And it got worse after her death because I could not live up to what she expected of me in connection with her illness.

My heavy guilt

Even before my mother received a lung cancer diagnosis, I had fearful thoughts about how it would go when my mother got old and sick and needed to have me there with her for longer periods of time.

When she was well, I always only visited her for two or three hours and only rarely. She had gotten used to that, even though she never understood why I could not stay longer without feeling very bad. I did not understand it myself, and I never told her because I did not want to hurt her.

The sicker she got, the angrier she became with me. Angry that I did not go with her to the various examinations at the hospital. Angry that I did not visit more often than I did. "You don't know how long you have me," she said. But I had promised myself that I would not risk getting sick with stress again at any cost. Nor did I want to risk having my sole proprietorship business fail because I did not spend enough time on it.

I am proud that, despite the huge pressure she put on me, I kept the agreement with myself. But at the same time, I am terribly sorry that my mother had to be alone so much and do without me, even though she was sick. For many years I was so burdened with guilt that I could not bear to hear the hymn 'Stay Close to Me' because she had just used that sentence in an attempt to make me stay. And I went home anyway.

The letter that released me

I worked for several years in different ways with my feelings of guilt in relation to my mother. A work I have described in my book: *See Yourself With Friendly Eyes*. But the blame for not being there when she died remained like a painful memory in the background of my consciousness. And sometimes it popped up and could flip my mood in an instant.

Only seven years after her death did I write a letter from my mother to me. A letter that made a huge difference.

I can still dream of my mother at night. The other day I dreamed that I was lying in her sickbed, holding her tenderly. I woke up feeling sad that this is not the way it happened. My feelings of guilt can also still make an appearance on my inner stage. But they no longer have the weight they had before.

The inspiration for the letter was rooted in painful longing. Here it comes:

"Dear Ilse,

Sorry I was so self-absorbed in the end – and angry with you. I know you did your best. That you also had children and grandchildren to take care of. But I just wanted you to be with me.

Sorry, I did not appreciate that you actually called once a week and lent me a friendly ear for a long time. I know listening to the conflicts I was involved in wore you down. Thank you for actually calling Hjørring Municipality and trying to get me what I wanted. Sorry I didn't want it after all when it was suddenly possible.

I know you are fragile, and your energy is limited. And that you are easily overstimulated. I can see that the situation was difficult for you, and that you did not have the energy to travel to Hjørring to be with me during the examinations. I just felt so let down.

Sorry, I threatened suicide. Sorry, I could never see you as you are. I know you would have liked to help me and that you did your best.

Love, Mum"

I found that the letter almost wrote itself. And that it felt incredibly real and releasing. I read it aloud to myself in front of a picture my mother had painted, while the tears flowed.

To my great surprise, I felt that the heavy guilt I had been feeling practically disappeared within a few days, and I could instead feel love for my mother. It was a wonderful change. And it was completely unexpected. I guess I had thought that the letter would bring me relief, but I had been ready to carry the guilt for being absent during her final difficult moments for the rest of my life.
Instead, I now have the feeling that my mother is sending me love from her place in heaven. And it fills me with gratitude.

Our deceased relatives live in their essence

It should be apparent to all that when I use the word "heaven", I am not referring to the literal blue sky. Heaven is the Christian metaphor for the place where we go when we die.

People imagine many different things about life after death. Here, you will be presented with my beliefs, but first I just want to say that you do not need to see things the same way. You can certainly use ancestry therapy even if you do not think there is any life after death. Soon I will tell you how, but first here is a short description of how I see things.

I imagine that when we die, we leave the body and enter another world. On the threshold, we leave our fears, neuroses and the unfortunate self-protection strategies we are caught up in. We let go of the roles we have tried to fulfil and live on in our essence. This conviction was reinforced during my 11 years as a pastor, where I saw many dead people. Every time it seemed clear to me: The person who lived in this body is no longer here. The body is like a wax figure. Devoid of personality and life.

We live on in our essence. And in that state, we can see everything in a clearer light, the way the apostle Paul writes about eternal life in the First Epistle to the Corinthians in the New Testament:

"For now we see in a mirror dimly, but then face to face. Now I know in part; then I shall know fully, even as I have been fully known." (1 Chor. 13:12)

Here and now we see only fragments of the great reality. Most of us experience being present in our essence only briefly, after which we again lose ourselves in our everyday struggles, worries or chores.

After death we live in our essence. Here we will be able to grasp the meaning of everything and understand the whole context. So even if your relative was never able to see you as you are, it will be possible for her after death, when she has hung up all her veils and is free of fear.

For those of you with other beliefs

Perhaps you do not expect life after death. Writing letters can be a relief, even if you see your letters as just fantasy. Not unlike the way you can feel relief when the hero in a movie is set free, even though you know it is not real. You might even cry with him when he reunites with someone he loves, and something can also happen inside you.

If you contact and talk to your own inner image of a relative, even more can happen than when watching movies. You will be involved on a personal level to a greater degree, and there may be a reconciliation that blows a breath of peace and calm throughout your psyche.

When I write to myself from my deceased mother, picture it as though I am sending an image – a projection of my mother – into the universe. I imagine that she lives there in her essence and can express love without reservation. Facing this version of my mother, I feel inward and contact the deepest wishes I have that relate to her. And then I write the letter from her to me. You can use your imagination and treat it like a game.

Ancestry therapy in relation to living and deceased relatives

Above, you saw an example of a letter from my mother, a deceased relative. Most people find it easier to imagine their relative being present in her essence when that relative is deceased. In the upcoming chapter, you will find several examples of letters from deceased relatives. The chapter is about grandparents. I have mostly used my own examples, and all my grandparents have passed away.

In the following chapters, you will also find examples of letters from relatives who are still alive. Here you can see how it is possible to imagine your living relatives being present in their essence – a state where they have greater awareness and wisdom than they can normally tap into.

When I realised the effectiveness of this method, I decided to write this book. I hope it will inspire you to renew your relationship with your parents and grandparents – actually, with your entire ancestry – so that you can feel like they are behind you, supporting you, more than they are today.

Enjoy,

Ilse Sand, Hald Hovedgaard

CHAPTER 1

Get support from your grandparents

Your parents are most important. First and foremost, you need to get their backing and recognition. However, your emotional reactions will probably be strongest in relation to them, and if you are overwhelmed by emotions, it can be difficult to learn a new method.

So, consider starting with one of your grandparents.

The importance of grandparents

Perhaps you have or had a warm emotional relationship with your parents' parents, perhaps it is, or was, at arm's length, or perhaps you never got to know them. No matter the relationship you have or had with them, they probably play a bigger part in your life than you might think. You carry their genes, and they live through your parents, who in turn left their imprint on you. Therefore, your grandparents are a very important part of how you became who you are.

Even if they fail to give you their full support or if they died before they managed to give you everything they had, there is still time. This is one of the most significant benefits of ancestry therapy.

The contact I had with my grandparents while they were alive was not particularly deep. In fact, my emotional attachment to them was so shallow that I did not shed a tear at any of the four funerals, even though I normally cry easily. If you feel the same way about one or more of your grandparents, this will not stop you from gaining something positive from them now.

Letter from my grandmother

I started by writing to myself from the grandparents that I most see myself in. My grandmother was introverted and sensitive, and she loved peace and quiet and low-key activities. My grandfather, on the other hand, was extremely outgoing and incredibly popular and loved to invite everyone he met home for coffee. Most people saw my grandfather as the happy and always hospitable ideal man, who unfortunately was married to a sad and boring wife.

When my grandmother grew old, she fell ill with arthritis, and by the end, she could not turn her head anymore. She did not have a way with kids, nor did she have the energy to show interest in us grandchildren. But the two of us observed each other from a distance.

When I set out to write a letter from her, I had no idea what would come out of it. But in 15 minutes, I had created a letter which I think will make me happy for the rest of my life. Here it is:

> *"Dear Ilse,*
>
> *I am glad to see that you care about animals as much as I did. All in all, you resemble me. You are just as sensitive and fragile, and you are easily overwhelmed and need to retreat.*
>
> *I am pleased to see that you have – and that you take – the chances and opportunities I didn't have.*
>
> *Everyone expected of me that I would be there and act as host every time your grandfather dragged guests home and ruined my peace. And I dared not say no. Instead, I grew bitter and sick, and your mother, and thus also you, suffered because of it.*
>
> *I am really happy to see that you are saying no and taking care of yourself. I am pleased that you are using your sensitive side creatively. Continue to take good care of yourself, Ilse. You have overcome many challenges, and you will also get through old age just fine. All my best wishes and thoughts.*
>
> *Love from your grandmother, Ellen"*

It surprised me how touched and happy I became with her comforting words about coping with ageing. She had done that herself. She actually lived to the age of 85, and towards the end she got to live a quieter life, the way she wanted.

I was also moved by a sense of solidarity with her. We are made of the same fabric, she and I, and she walked this path before I did.

Letter from my grandfather

My grandfather died when I was 11 years old. I especially remember that he loved pulling me up on his lap and holding me. I did not like that and tried to wrench myself free without being rude. He was a quiet man, who would drop by to help my father whitewash walls at the farm. I remember him walking with a lime bucket and broom. When I set out to let him write a letter to me, the letter flowed easily and effortlessly through my fingers.

> *"Dear Sweet Ilse,*
>
> *I did not understand children. I just liked you so much. You were so small and delicate and pretty and smart. And I loved sitting with you on my knee – and I did not much like letting go. Now I can see that you needed something else from me. I now wish I had known how to support children.*
>
> *I am glad to see that you are doing well after all. And proud that you are my granddaughter.*
>
> *I wish you the very best.*
>
> *Love from your grandfather, Christian"*

After writing the letter and reading it a few times, I felt a little richer. As if I had received his blessing to live my life as best I can.

A liberating realisation of powerlessness

I love that my grandfather writes about what he would wish. None of us manage to only pass on the good things.

When my grandfather lived, they did not have the knowledge we have today about what benefits children. And in 30 years' time, we will know even more. And perhaps we will discover that some of the things we are doing right now do more harm than good. But each of us acts based on the knowledge we have now and on what we think is best.

With hindsight, I see a lot that I now wish I could have done better. For example, there are situations with my children where I did not behave constructively or just fell short. Using the word "wish" helps me express the feeling of powerlessness inherent in the fact that past actions cannot be undone. And to recognise your powerlessness can in itself be releasing, both for the one who feels it and the one to whom you are acknowledging it.

Perhaps there is something that your relatives wish they could have done or known. They each probably have or had their own struggles where they are trying or tried to survive with the means and opportunities at their disposal.

If you let them write you a letter, you give them the chance to remedy the things they did that left marks, as well as the things they never passed on and which left their descendants with the inner feeling that they are missing something.

When the letter does not write itself

When I decided to write from my grandfather on my mother's side, I got stuck. There was no inspiration. But I knew he was important, and I did not want to give up so easily. I therefore decided to begin by writing a letter from myself to him. I tried to be completely honest, with no censorship. Here is my letter:

> *"Dear Grandfather,*
>
> *It's hard for me to write to you. You were very important, and I admired you from a distance. But I do not remember ever feeling either seen or heard by you. You were more interested in my cousins and in my sister, who was more talkative than me. I never knew what you thought of me.*
>
> *Mum once said that you thought I felt too sorry for myself about their divorce. And when I called and told you that I had been given a permanent priesthood, you were really surprised. You didn't expect anyone to hire me.*
>
> *But I am the one who has walked in your footsteps the most. I give lectures, like you did, I write books, like you did, and I am involved in the community, the way you were. I create something new, just like you did.*

Thank you for staying in good spirits and continuing to ride around on your tricycle until you passed away at the age of 99. It gives me hope that I may be able to do something similar. I hope you are in a nice place now.

Love from your granddaughter, Ilse"

It felt good to say that to him. And that is when I felt the inspiration to write a letter the other way:

"Dear Ilse,

I'm sorry I didn't take the time to get to know you. I did not care about children until I could have a sensible conversation with them. And when you became a teenager, you seemed sad and timid. You were often silent and sat watching the rest of us. I did not like that.

I was surprised when you chose to study theology and involve yourself with church life, which I had been involved with for many years. Do you remember I gave you the multi-volume work Bibelen i kulturhistorisk lys (the Bible from a cultural-historic perspective)?

I really enjoyed telling you about the pastors I loved, and I hoped you would want to become like one of them. But there was something introverted about you that worried me.

Now I can see that you are doing things well your way. You use your talents in a different way than I did, and I have to admit that it works out great. Now I am delighted to see how you fight and develop and help others.

> *Sending you my best thoughts and wishes. Love from your grandfather, Christian Ulrik"*

Seize the chance to speak out

When I had written both letters, I had the nice sensation of having talked things out with my grandfather. When I meet him in heaven, it will be without reservation on my part. They faded away with the letters. And even if you do not expect to meet your deceased relatives again, a reservation that fades away will in itself have a balancing effect on your psyche. You will then be able to think of your relative without wincing on the inside or disturbing your inner peace.

In real life, it is not always possible to talk things out fully. It requires that both parties dare admit their mistakes, and that they can accommodate their own as well the other person's sorrow or anger. If we cannot stand to listen to each other about our feelings, then whatever one party has to say can easily be perceived as hurtful by the other. This ends up with mud-flinging or with one party beating a hasty retreat.

When using the tools of ancestry therapy, you only need to be able to accommodate your own emotions. In the letters, you can say everything you need – and you can get the answer you most want.

A letter from someone who does not resemble you

I considered skipping my grandmother on my father's side. I thought a letter from her would probably not tell me anything, since I did not think we were anything alike. She was full of energy and incredibly active and often noisy. But I decided to give the letter a try:

"Dear Ilse,

I didn't want to feel myself and everything I was ashamed of. I wanted to be with someone who had a high energy level and who could make me laugh. Your sister could. She resembles me, and we have good chemistry. You were more cautious and restrained, which simply did not resonate with me.

When I see you now, I am nonetheless proud to be your grandmother. You have surprised me. Imagine that little Ilse could spread her books all over the world. If someone had told me that one of my grandchildren would do so, I would have been sure it would be your sister. You were probably the last one I would have guessed.

But you have apparently had something in you that I overlooked. Now I welcome the positive surprise, and I follow your life with pride.

Love from your grandmother, Agnes"

My reaction to my grandmother's letter came as a surprise to me. Quite simply, it affected me on a deeper level than I had expected. It was a relief to be told that she looks upon me positively now. And the fact that she is actually proud of me makes me happy. Instead of a grumpy feeling of being overlooked, I now feel gratitude because she can finally see me and wishes me well.

Even though, at first, I didn't feel like writing to my grandmother and grandfather, I'm glad I did. They were both extremely physically active, and as I write to them, this feels contagious. Perhaps I have some of those genes somewhere as well.

What if you don't have any good memories?

If you cannot remember the slightest good thing about one of your grandparents, and if you have not been told anything positive about her, you might think that there is nothing to gain from writing a letter from her. But even if you only feel negative emotions, the effect of the letter may surprise you. A letter can, after all, just be a series of sentences, all of which begin with "Sorry, …"

Perhaps the following examples of apologies from grandparents will inspire you:

> *You should know that I deeply regret not showing more interest in my grandchildren and thus in you. I don't know how to explain it, but for me, kids were just there. I didn't think of talking to you. Please forgive me.*
>
> *Grandfather*

I know you didn't like talking about your mother. I wish I could have kept my curiosity under control. You told me that your mother never went out and that you worried a lot. But instead of being caring, I plucked you for answers like a hen with all my questions. My little Jane, I should have just asked my son, your father, and left you out of it. I hope you can forgive me.

Grandmother

Your little brother was more fragile and much easier for me to love than you were. In hindsight, I feel it was so wrong. It was by no means OK of me to treat you differently.

Grandmother

Even if you have no positive expectations, I recommend that you test the ancestry therapy tools in relation to all of your grandparents. The more frail or un-tapped your relationship with them, the greater the reason for correcting it. And something might pop up that you did not expect.

Here are some examples of support and recognition from grandparents:

Thank you for visiting me, even though we were not very close.

Grandfather

You have always been a very thoughtful and caring person, even when you were a little girl.

Grandmother

Lena, you need to know that I loved you very much. You were a little ray of sunshine in our family. You brightened the mood, and it was just great.

Grandfather

In the above example, Lena did not know her grandfather. He had passed away when she was only one year old. She could not remember him but had been told a little about him. She recounts:

Actually I had thought that a letter to my grandfather would be quite short. But when I started the letter, more and more things came out, so it has been much more rewarding than I assumed beforehand. It amazes and confirms to me that writing can do something very special – as opposed to just mulling over things in your head.

Lena

Lena found that after writing the letter she cared more about her grandfather.

Feel your connection to your ancestry

I had no emotional contact to my grandparents while they were alive. And it was as if my doubts whether they liked me at all had quashed my interest in their parents and prevented me from feeling connected with my kin. I had not thought of it as a shortcoming before. But when I wrote a letter to myself from all four of them, I sensed that I felt a deeper connection – also with relatives going further back in my lineage.

Since I was a teenager, I have been desperate for a sense of belonging. Several times in my life I stayed in relationships that were no longer right for me for far too long because I could not let go of the feeling of being connected. On occasion, I had this idea, which provoked anxiety, that if I left the relationship, I would be completely unattached to anything or anyone and drift into nothingness and disappear.

After working with ancestry therapy, I find that I belong to the living and the dead of my kin, and therefore, I feel much more resilient when it comes to losing relationships or the sense of belonging. I have found a foundation, an anchor, in a context of people whose genes are similar to mine.

The main points in Chapter 1: Get support from your grandparents

- Your grandparents have probably influenced you more than you might ordinarily think.
- You can help them if they did not manage to give you everything they had or if they are unable to give you very much.
- You may be surprised by your own emotional reaction to receiving a letter, even if you have written it yourself.
- The word "wish" is good when you want to express powerlessness. If you find it difficult to start writing the

letter to yourself, it might help to start writing a letter the other way. A letter *from* you *to* your relative.

- In real life, it is not always possible to talk things out. But entirely new things are possible when you use ancestry therapy.

- If you work comprehensively with the method, you will probably find that you are better anchored to your kin, and because of this, you will experience a greater sense of support from your ancestors.

CHAPTER 2

Letters from and to your parents

If your parents are still alive, you have the opportunity to say what you need to say to them and ask for their recognition. But not everyone's relationship to their parents is comfortable enough to allow for complete honesty and directness. Ancestry therapy is a good alternative here. The same applies, of course, if they are no longer alive.

In this chapter, you will see a number of examples of letters *to* and *from* parents.

I get a sense of peace from the letter to my mother

In the book's introduction, you read the releasing letter I wrote to myself from my mother. In it, she apologised that she had not been able to see me and had not appreciated me for what I had done for her. After the letter had time to settle, I could write a new and more loving letter to her. As previously mentioned, I have written several angry letters that she never saw. Perhaps they prepared me for being able to write this letter from my heart and from the source of the sorrow.

I tried to be completely honest, with no censorship.

"Dear Mum,

I do not know if I miss you. I am most of all relieved that the two of us no longer have to be tormented by being in a relationship that is not working. I wish I could have done better.

I don't remember that looking you in the eyes ever felt good. It wasn't me you saw. What you saw, you wanted to change. You looked at me with reservations. I so wish I could've seen joy in your eyes when you looked at me.

Neither did you like the way I looked at you, Mum. I saw a neglected child. A fragile, disjointed person who could not contain her feelings and therefore acted them all out. I saw your loneliness.

I don't know if I've ever loved you. As a child I admired you. You were so easy-going and clever and classy. When I compared you to the neighbours' wives, I thought you were a star and was proud to be your child.

At least it was good that you were happy when things went well for me. I would have liked to be able to tell you about what I have achieved today and to experience the joy you would have felt. You were happy both on my behalf and yours. You loved to boast of my achievements. And I enjoyed seeing you be happy because of this.

Thank you for pushing me to take an education.

By God I would have liked to help you. I would have loved to listen to your pain and stroke your hair. I would have liked to climb up in your bed when you were dying, to hold you and rock you in my arms. But you never liked me touching you.

We were probably just too different. Even though we resemble each other externally, we do not want the same thing. I want to be authentic, go into depth, seek the truth. You want to have fun. I could have learned something from that. You never wanted to think about anything that might spoil your mood. Instead, you'd rather play another game of cards.

You once said that you were sorry that you didn't do anything when I was a teenager and was lying about in bed a lot. But what should you have done? You couldn't give me the closeness I needed. No one had taught you. And at that time we didn't have the opportunities to get help that we have today. I think you did the best you could.

There was no way for us to meet, my dear Mum. It was just such a pity. The genuine contact that existed between us was thin and rare.

I look forward to meeting you in heaven without our shield of fear and self-protection and to see each other as we are. Until then, dear Mum, I hope that you are in a place where you can be bright and playful, which is when you are at your best.

Love, Ilse"

I took the letter to a psychotherapist and read it aloud and shared my grief. And I experienced that there was a place in me that had found peace, even though it was sad.

Here is another example:

Sarah heals her relationship with her father

Sarah had a complicated relationship with her father. To him it felt unnatural and awkward to express positive emotions. He had never done it – at least not for her. And the times when he had overlooked her, she had become very unhappy. One example is when she read on his Facebook page that the whole family had been gathered for his birthday – and she had not been there. Or when he forgot to answer her question if she could come to visit during Christmas. Throughout her life, she had been unsure if she had any particular significance to him.

When I met Sarah at my practice, she had written many angry letters to her father throughout her life. And at times she had chosen not to be with him because she could not handle the hurt feelings she felt when she was near him.

I suggested that she write a letter the other way, i.e. from her father to her. A letter that would make her so happy that she would feel released in relation to him. Sarah later said that she had written the letter very quickly. In fact, somewhere deep inside, she had known for years what that letter had to contain. And she was deeply touched when she read it afterwards.

Here is Sarah's letter:

"Dear Sara,

I know you are the one who has always loved me the most. Even though I did not treat you very well, you loved me and continued to love me. And I know you still love me. And that if I just show the slightest interest, you drop everything to be with me.

It doesn't matter that we don't see each other so often. I can feel in my heart that you think of me. I am happy you resemble me. Your intelligence, your sensitivity, your personal strength and your endurance. You can allow yourself to be very picky when you find a partner. And if someone does not treat you as you deserve, I will come after them. You deserve the best, my dear child.

The two of us will always belong together. When I am dead, I will look at you lovingly from heaven and rejoice when things go well for you. And I will send you my deepest compassion when you struggle and suffer.

The most loving greetings from your father, forever"

When Sarah and I next met, she told me that a few days after our last meeting she began feeling deep joy and realised that the time for anger had passed. Instead, she wanted to write to her father from a loving place inside herself. When she did so, it arose strong positive emotions that were unfamiliar to her and that she could barely handle.

Here is the letter:

"Dear Dad,

Thank you for allowing me to love you. There was something nice and beautiful between the two of us. I think that, sometimes, you also felt that being with me was like heaven.

I loved you as much as a child can love someone. And I still love you. And I will allow myself to feel that fully. I feel this wonderful warmth in my chest. It is not mine and not yours, but something that occurs when we are together and sometimes when I think of you.

Dad, I sense your distress and your sensitivity. The things you don't want to acknowledge. I also see your format. You know how to be what the wise musician Peter Bastian calls 'being an adult'. You carry the weight of your own emotional life without bothering others with it. Thank you for bearing your guilt yourself and not burdening us children.

Thank you for the security you gave me when I was small. Thank you for the times you defended me against Marie, even though it cost you dearly.

There are many things I wanted to do with you – the two of us alone. But I don't want to ask. It would cause you problems in relation to Sonja, and you don't need to have alone-time with me. And I would find it very difficult to handle rejection. It would send me right back to my childhood hell, where I begged and asked you if we could be alone together just for a while, and you got annoyed and angry.

But maybe one day I might be lucky and meet you alone at home. Then I would really like to sit next to you by the window and look at the birds on your bird feeder. Without saying anything. Just sit there – the two of us – looking in the same direction, resembling each other, and listening together. But maybe you are unable to relax at all because you will be afraid that I will talk about feelings. Maybe you even asked Sonja to stay close by your side when I'm visiting so you can avoid it.

Fortunately, we have good conversations on the phone. And if you pass away before we get the chance to sit together looking at birds, I can live with it.

You hope that you will drop dead suddenly, without pain. I hope for you that this is how it will happen. But I also hope for myself that I will have the opportunity to say goodbye. Sit by your bed and hold your hand. And I hope that you will meet Grandfather and Grandmother in heaven.

Love from your daughter, Sarah"

When we met afterwards, Sarah initially left the letter in her bag. She was very hesitant to read it out but decided to do so anyway. While she was reading, she was overwhelmed by her feelings and had to take a break several times. The room was filled with love and warmth. After that she sat there circling her hands around in the air as though she had no idea how to coexist with those strong emotions. I confirmed again and again that her feelings are beautiful, heartfelt and natural. That they are not dangerous and are allowed to exist. Eventually she calmed down. A few weeks later, she told me that a fearful feeling, which she often had and had been wondering about – a feeling that her emotions could grow too large and would blow her apart – had disappeared.

Although her father knew nothing about the letters, he could probably sense that something in their relationship had changed. Because a week later, when they met for a family birthday party, he sat beside her and did something that was unusual for him. He took her hand and held it warmly under the table. No one else saw that they were holding hands. How long they sat like that, she did not know. It was as if time stood still. She tried to participate in the conversation, but her attention was in her heart, where she felt a warm stream of happiness. "If I had not first practised containing the strong feelings with the letters, I would probably have fled or maybe become embarrassed. But I just sat there and enjoyed the warm stream, which felt healing and reminded me of when I was a child and when my relation to my father was at its happiest."

After that experience, Sarah's anger and bitterness toward her father evaporated. Now she feels a deep gratitude because he taught her about love and happiness. Experiences that live within her and that will continue to bring her joy – even after he passes away.

Sarah's experience of release is one among many I have witnessed. Here are a few more examples:

Lena gets good advice from her father

While Lena was writing the letter to herself from her late father, she could suddenly sense what advice he would have for her. And even though she wrote it herself, it felt like she was hearing his voice:

> *"Lena, accept that life has left its mark. The life you lived has given you a lot of experiences and scars, but you are still alive, and so you can continue to make choices as you see fit."*

And:

> *"Lena, remember that you should never be the one who is responsible for your mother's happiness."*

These were two pieces of advice that Lena wanted to reflect on and consider – could they bring something new into her life?

The feeling of loving care for "Little Jane" was awakened in Jane

Jane had not had contact with her mother for seven years. Her mother was mentally ill and had rejected her. But her mother still took up too much of Jane's mind. Jane was angry, and no one wanted to hear about that. Not even the man she had been married to for 45 years. Her friends had encouraged her to try to forget her terrible family and find something positive to think of.

In the letter Jane wrote to herself from her mother, there were apologies for the numerous times she was let down. Here are some quotes from her mother's letter:

> *"I should have walked with you on your first day of school, and of course, I should have held your hand when you were hospitalised alone with appendicitis."*

> *"You looked right through me, and then I punished you. I should have asked for help instead."*

> *"You ran off to Copenhagen at the young age of 17. How I wish I had come with you in the car and waved with Dad at the train and blown you lots of kisses along the way. I'm so sorry that I stayed at home in anger and waved goodbye from the doorway saying: 'If you regret it, don't come home.'"*

> *"You got a shock when you came home to attend your father's funeral, and I was lying under the duvet. The bouquet and the rose for the man I loved stood in the bathroom. Dad should have been in a zinc coffin because he had been in the water for six weeks, and I could not afford it. So that's why I cancelled the funeral. I could have asked for help instead."*

In addition to the apologetic passages, a small selection of which you read above, the letter also thanked Jane for all the good things she had done for her mother. For example, Jane had found her mother a new husband by placing a personal ad, and she brought her mother lots of joy by giving birth to two sweet girls. In general, Jane had come to her mother's aid countless times over many years.

When Jane subsequently read the letter to her husband, they both wept. Jane was surprised and shocked by the number of times she was let down and the severity of these incidents, which had popped up in the letter. She suddenly saw how much Little Jane had had to bear alone. Her mother had been unable to listen to Jane and contain her feelings. And her mother had been too fragile to bear her own responsibility. In the letter, when her mother finally took responsibility for her guilt, Jane noticed that the baggage of heavy emotions she had been carrying since childhood had suddenly become a lot lighter.

After this letter, Jane was entirely resolved that she would never see her mother again, and instead, she focused her care on the child within herself. The child who had tried to cope with the impossible.

The main points in Chapter 2: Letters from and to your parents

- Getting a loving letter from a parent can open up a wealth of positive emotions, even if you have written it yourself.
- You might also get some good advice from the parent you're writing from.
- When a parent takes responsibility for letting a child down, the child becomes able to feel the weight of the responsibility and guilt she has been carrying, which in reality belongs to someone else.

CHAPTER 3

Preparing yourself to write

You probably have already started to think about how you will write your own letters. In this chapter, you will get concrete advice about the writing situation and how to get started. This advice applies whether you write *to* or *from* your relative.

Choose one relative at a time

As previously mentioned, it may be a good idea to start with a relative with whom you have an uncomplicated relationship, so that trying ancestry therapy for the first time does not overwhelm you with emotions.

It is best to concentrate on one relative at a time and let some time pass between each instance. You might need half a day or several days to let one letter settle and the other begin to sprout. If you decide to write to several relatives in quick succession, the letters may become too superficial.

Once you have chosen the person you want to start with, it may be good to leave her in your consciousness for a few days. Many people find that while they mull over the task, the process suddenly starts on its own. Words begin to appear. A letter knocks at the door. And then you just need to make time to write as quickly as possible.

Should you start writing *to* or *from* your relative?

Most people find that it is the letter *from* the relative that has the greatest sense of release, so I suggest that you start with that if you can. Enjoy letting your relative give you something good.

In some cases, the *from* letter offers such a profound sense of release that no additional letters are needed.

Another advantage of starting with *from* is that a loving letter from your relative can create an opening in you, allowing you to feel a vulnerability and perhaps some positive emotions that have been hidden behind a shield. If you also want to write a letter *to* the relative you wrote from, you can probably do it afterwards from a place that is rooted more deeply in your heart. This is what happened to Lena, which you can read about below:

> *"Once I had written the letter to myself from my late father, I felt more than just disappointment and anger towards him for the first time. I also felt love. I find it strange that words I wrote could become so vivid and so real that I found myself relaxing my shoulders and let me feel the sympathy I had for my father as well as sorrow that we didn't share more love while he was alive."*
>
> *Lena*

If it is difficult to write the letter *from*, or if it just feels more natural to start writing *to*, you can certainly do that. Perhaps there are negative feelings at stake that need to be aired before there can be room for receiving something good from your relative.

If writing letters one way doesn't work, try the other. Once you get started, you can do it several times. You can choose to start by writing *to* your relative and then writing *from* your relative and to yourself. After that, you may want to write a new letter *to* your relative. A letter that is more peaceful than the first.

The letter *to* and the letter *from* do not have to be aligned. You may feel the need to let one letter be an answer to the other. Maybe you would rather write something completely different. Once you have chosen which letter you want to start with, you are ready to proceed.

Create a good environment

Make sure you have a quiet moment, without disturbance. It might be a good idea to be alone, so you can weep if you need to. Do it somewhere that helps you think big. For example, sit somewhere with a beautiful view, under a lush tree, in front of the fireplace or in front of a candle.

If you are one of those people who have a hard time writing by hand, just use your computer. But otherwise, I suggest you write the letters by hand. When you do that, you slow the pace, and that's good when you want to go deeper. In addition, writing by hand makes it possible to work far away from your mobile and computer, and in that way, it helps avoid disturbances. Another advantage of writing by hand is that, when you write the letters, it is better to look at a piece of paper or out through the window than into a screen.

Get ready to go into depth with yourself

Before you start writing, you may benefit from spending a few minutes to get in the right mood. Maybe you need to listen to some music. Sit down and feel the way the chair carries you. Let your attention wander to your feet and to your hands. Also let the attention shine like a sun on your face. Make some grimaces by stretching your facial skin in different directions, and then let your jaw hang loose. Breathe all the air out of your lungs and then let yourself take a few deep breaths. Now you are probably ready to get started.

In Chapters Four and Five, you can find more instructions on how to write letters *from* and *to*, respectively.

The main points in Chapter 3: Preparing yourself to write

- It may be a good idea to start by testing the tools of ancestry therapy in relation to a relative towards whom you do not have particularly strong feelings.

- Give each relative space to fill your consciousness for a few hours or a few days before you start writing the letter.

- There are advantages to begin by writing to yourself, but in some situations, it works best to start writing to her.

- Create a nice environment for your writing.

- Take the time to establish good contact with your body and with yourself before you start writing.

CHAPTER 4

How to write letters to yourself

This chapter offers ideas on how to write a letter to yourself from your relative. And what you can do if hurt feelings get in your way.

You have probably tried writing a letter to someone else. But, as previously mentioned, writing from someone else to you can feel artificial or staged. You may feel a reluctance to start the task. But if you get started, you will probably be surprised by how easy it is – like Lena in the example below.

> *When I was given the task of writing a letter to myself from my late father, my first thought was that it was really strange. I was quite sceptical and had low expectations, but I thought: "Well, OK – let's see what I can get out of it."*
>
> *Once I sat down in front of the white sheet of paper, it went much easier than I had expected. And several times along the way I thought: "Hey, where did this come from?"*
>
> *Lena*

You will probably experience something similar if you give it a try.

How to imagine the person you are writing from

When you write to yourself from a relative, imagine that she looks at you with loving eyes. For some people, it is easy to envision this. Others have to work on it a little more. If you are in the latter group, it is probably because you have not seen her loving gaze very often. Perhaps you have never heard her express her feelings from the deeper layers of her heart. Perhaps she has completely lost touch with her own essence. At some point in her life, she may have frozen in fear – perhaps in a situation she no longer remembers – and, therefore, she cannot step in front of her shield and be truly genuine and emotionally present with you. Perhaps her past trauma has left her behind veil after veil of self-protection strategies, so that she cannot understand herself or see you for who you are.

Try to ignore the troublesome parts of your relative when you write the letter to yourself. If she is stubborn or inflexible, it is probably because of fear. Imagine that she is talking to you from a place in herself where she is unspoiled by her own trauma, from somewhere deep within and from her heart.

For some of you, it may be helpful to imagine that your relative is deceased. Others would rather imagine that the person is near-death or that she has woken up in the middle of the night with temporary lucidity.

You should preferably avoid empathising with your relative's traumas and pain too deeply. The exercise is first and foremost about feeling your own longing. Imagine that she is in a place inside herself where there is light and clarity, as if she woke up in the middle of the night with an insight she does not normally have.

Your actual letter

Tune yourself into writing something you will be happy to read. Just start writing what comes to mind. If you need inspiration, one or more of the questions in the list below will probably help you:

Maybe it will make you happy if she:

- Appreciates a side of you, and if so, which one?
- Gives you an apology for something she has said or done, and if so, what?
- Writes that she knows you've always loved her?
- Writes that she wishes she could have done something better, and if so, what?
- Suggests something she would like to do with you, and if so, what?
- Says that you are very important to her?
- Writes that she knows that one of her actions hurt you?
- Talks about something she has regretted?
- Says she loves you?

- Thanks you for something you have done (what?) or for who you are?
- Says she is proud of you or of something you do?
- Suggests that you work to make your relationship closer?
- Confirms that something you do is good?
- Appreciates that you are different from her or that the two of you disagree?
- Wishes you the very best?
- Gives you good advice in the situation you are currently in?

Hurt feelings can stand in the way

If you are filled with negative thoughts and hurt feelings in relation to the person you want to write from, the letter might not end up having that releasing effect.

Perhaps your relative does not know how to listen to you. Or maybe she is stuck in the pitfall called extremely low self-esteem, where she has lost connection to self-love and thus also to her ability to love you. As Susanna's father exclaimed when, after several years of attempts, she finally managed to get through to him with the message that she missed him: "I didn't think I had anything anyone could miss."

If you bear a negative image of your relative, try to soften it so that she becomes more human. See her in front of you as she was when she was a year old and fumbled her way through life.

Think of what she has suffered. Perhaps she did her best based on the knowledge and opportunities she had at that time.

Anger about your childhood pain

If your childhood was painful or void of joy, you may bear anger against one of your parents because of it. Remember that the dysfunction or lack of parental competence you suffered has roots stretching far back in your ancestry. It is not just the fault of one or both of your parents. Quite the contrary, they are themselves burdened by the weight of their ancestors.

As mentioned before, directing your anger towards your entire ancestry rather than just one parent can lighten your relationship with that parent or grandparent. This might provide the opening inside you that is necessary to enable you to receive something healing from your ancestor.

One day you will be strong enough to dare to feel deep enough into the anger to sense the following feelings, which are often hidden underneath: Powerlessness, helplessness, despair, sorrow and pain – but also compassion – both with respect to yourself and to your relatives. When you achieve this, you will not only heal yourself but also your kin. The reconciliation and peace that you create will be propagated in future generations.

The main points in Chapter 4: How to write letters to yourself

- Imagine that the relative you are writing from looks upon you lovingly.
- You can use an inspirational list of questions if you need help starting the process.
- Hurt feelings can stand in the way. They can often be softened up.
- If you direct your anger at the pain of your childhood to your entire ancestry, rather than on only one of your closest ancestors, you create an opportunity for something new to happen.

CHAPTER 5

How to write a letter to your ancestor

Maybe you already have experience writing a letter *from* your relative *to* yourself. Or maybe you are one of those people who prefer to start writing *from* yourself *to* her.

In the last chapter, I described how you should imagine that the person you write *from* is present in her essence, where she has a deeper understanding. When you write *to* your relative, there are two options. Either you can write to her as if she is in her essence, or you can relate to her as you see or remember her. Do what feels most natural. Maybe you will end up somewhere in between.

If you have never met her, you may still imagine who she was. This is the vision you should have in your inner eye as you write.

When you write *to*, you can let all your hurt feelings loose. Just turn off all censorship and release all your emotions.

When you're ready, you just need a good environment, with peace and quiet and plenty of time. Consider finding a picture. Inhale and exhale deeply a few times and find your peace and contact with yourself and your body, as described in Chapter Three. Then look at the picture or imagine the person in your mind's eye and feel inside yourself. What does it do to you emotionally to look at this person?

Maybe you need to sit still in front of the picture for a long time. Or maybe you should leave the picture and return to it a few times until it feels right to start writing.

A farewell letter

You can choose to write the letter as a farewell letter. In a farewell, the meaning of a relationship becomes more apparent, and the feelings are often clearer. If you imagine that your relative is dead or that, for one reason or another, you will never see them again, completely new feelings may emerge. These could be positive feelings towards her that you did not realise you had. Perhaps there will be room for them in a farewell because you do not have to be afraid of her reaction to your letter and because she can no longer pressure you. When you imagine that you are writing a final goodbye, you may find a sense of security and experience greater inner freedom to sense yourself on a deeper level and perhaps feel what you are going to miss.

If your relative is deceased, then a farewell letter is the obvious choice. If she is alive, you can consider whether a farewell letter could be a possibility. If it feels better writing an ordinary letter, just do that.

A letter that should not be sent, but that you write solely for your own sake, is an opportunity to air some of the feelings that are difficult to talk about in real life. For example:

> *Mum, I haven't always felt seen by you for who I am. I wish you asked me more questions – not only about what I have experienced and done – but also about who I am, how I feel and what I want deep inside.*

> *Dad, I get sad when you praise my sister for good marks in her exams. I can see you beaming with pride, and it stings my heart.*

Know your feelings

When you see your relative in your mind's eye, you may feel many different feelings, and it can be difficult to sort out what is what.

In the following, I describe how you can distinguish one feeling from the other. When you know exactly what feeling is currently occupying your inner stage, you can better figure out what you need to write or do.

You can distinguish between *basic feelings* and *mixed feelings*. A basic feeling can be registered in people from all cultures and nations and in higher animal species. All other feelings can be explained as different mixtures of the basic feelings. There is disagreement as to which feelings should be regarded as basic feelings. However, all psychologists agree on the following four:

1. Anger
2. Joy
3. Fear/Anxiety
4. Sadness/Sorrow

Most other feelings are a mixture of two or more of these feelings. Despair, for example, is a mixture of sorrow, anxiety and perhaps anger. Disappointment is a mixture of sorrow and anger. Jealousy is a mixture of fear and anger. Feeling excited is a mixture of joy and anxiety.

You feel your feelings in different degrees. The mildest degree of anger means that you sense that there is something you do not like. It can grow into irritation, anger or rage. Being "sad" in its weakest form can be felt as mild fatigue, and it can grow into a deep unhappiness. Fear or anxiety can manifest as mild unrest, which can grow into restlessness, and in its strongest form can be experienced as dizziness or as galloping palpitations. And joy can be experienced as a slight increase in energy and can grow into a euphoric experience filled with laughter, where your entire body is smiling.

If you are unsure which basic feelings are part of what you feel, you can use your thoughts as a guide. Feelings and thoughts are closely connected, so if it is easier for you to access your thoughts, you can zero in on your feelings that way.

Typical thoughts during anger

This is unfair
I'm being cheated/let down
She ought to be ashamed of herself
She should have thought more about me (moral judgement)
I should have discovered it sooner (moral judgement turned against yourself = internally focused anger)

Typical thoughts when feeling sadness

I would have liked …
I had been looking forward to …
I miss …
I wish …
I would have liked to keep …
I would have liked to be …

Typical thoughts when feeling joy

I am so lucky
This is so beautiful
What a wonderful day
Tomorrow will probably be even better
Good thing it did not get any worse

Typical thoughts when feeling anxiety

That will not turn out well
I can't stand it
I can't handle it
I will not make it
It's dangerous
It can go wrong

Be aware that what you feel is likely to be a mixture of several emotions, and your thoughts will probably reflect this. Maybe you are 90% angry and 10% sad – or vice versa. Or maybe you are 80% happy and 20% afraid. The better you know yourself on the inside, the better you can express what you feel.

It can be a relief to name your feelings. Sometimes a feeling loses all its intensity when recognised and expressed. Like the monster in the fairy tale that loses its power when someone guesses its name, a feeling can seem much more reliable and more like a friend when you get to know it better.

If you are mostly full of anger, there may be several reasons for this. One of them may be that your relative has treated you in a way you do not like. Anger is sometimes a signal that something is going on or has happened that you do not want to participate in. In that case, you may need to speak out or write an angry letter, where you can air your negative feelings.

If you have previously smouldered inside with anger, it is especially important to let it be expressed. You do not have to express it directly to the person unless something is going on between you that you want to stop. Otherwise, there may be advantages to just letting it flow into a letter that you do not send.

Another possibility is to see the anger as what it often is, namely a shield.

Anger is often the top layer

Often anger covers other more vulnerable emotions. If you dare feel them, something new may happen. Ask yourself, if your anger may be covering up:

Sorrow?
A feeling of helplessness?
Longing?
A vulnerable and unsafe place in yourself where you don't know what to do?

If you get in touch with a layer under the anger, you will gain access to a new way to contact the other person in the relationship you are working on. Anger leads to distance, while grief opens the heart.

Instead of: "Dad, I am so angry that you are overlooking me", you can try to formulate the vulnerability that exists underneath. For example:

- "Dad, I really want to be important to you."
- "Dad, I feel helpless in my attempt to establish a good relationship with you."
- "Dad, I feel deep sorrow that I cannot feel your love."
- "Dad, I would really like to feel a connection to you, but I feel rejected and powerless."
- "Dad, it doesn't feel like you can see me as I am. This makes me deeply unhappy."
- "Dad, I miss you."

If you can connect with the soft feelings underneath the anger, you can meet the person in the relationship you are working on with an open heart. And then something completely new is possible. An interaction is like a dance. If one of you begins to take new steps, the other can no longer continue the same way. And when you meet your relative from a vulnerable place, they are likely to have the courage to be more open and honest.

Be specific

When you start writing, it is important that you are very specific. So, for example, do not say: "I've always been …" but rather: "In that situation (for example, when you unexpectedly gave me a gift or when you forgot my birthday) I felt …" You get the most out of writing the letter if you write about specific events or situations.

If you find it difficult to feel what you need to write, you can probably find inspiration in a number of relevant questions, which you will find below:

What is the nice part of the relationship? What makes you happy? What would you like to say thank you for?
What is the unpleasant part of the relationship? What would you like to be free of?
What would you like to say thank you for?
What have you given in the relationship? (For example: "I think you were happy when I
…" Or: "I think your pain became less when I …")
What would you like to give more of?

Is there anything you have regretted?

How would you wish your relationship to be?

What would you wish you could do with the other person?

What do you miss in the relationship?

Is there anything you would like to apologise for?

What would you want for the other person?

Not all questions are relevant in all relationships, but *thank you* is important.

Thanks and my blessings

Remind yourself of the good experiences you had and of your relative's good intentions, even when what she did caused you or others pain. Even if you are mostly angry, it is good to try to find something to say thank you for.

If you cannot think of something good, you can always say thank you for what you learned; for example, from your shared experiences, from her absence or from your conflicts – even if the learning process was so painful that you would have preferred not to have done so. And when it comes to one of your ancestors, you can always thank them for your life. After all, you would not be here without them.

Good wishes for the other party are also important.

I hope you get …

I wish you to be …

If you open up to feel positive emotions and gratitude, you are on your way down the path of forgiveness. On the path to freeing yourself from the ties you have to the past. You might not quite be able to walk that path right now. But every time you gain the support of an ancestor, you may find that you become stronger and more flexible. For now, just do it to the best of your ability.

Control your need to explain

If what you are writing is not having much of an emotional impact, you may have started explaining too much. You may feel the urge to justify your feelings. A strong urge to explain says something about how uncertain you are about whether you are allowed to feel what you are feeling.

Explanations will not give you a sense of relief. Instead, tell your relative about the vulnerable feelings that underlie your need to explain. Then something completely new will probably happen. So, do not write: I feel like this because …. Instead, you could say: Right now, as I am writing to you, I feel uncertain whether you think I am OK.

Emotions cannot be either good or evil. They are just as they are. Everyone has many different kinds of feelings. This is quite natural, and you are always allowed to feel what you feel. No one is entitled to an explanation.

If the letter is to provide release, you need to talk about the feelings. Not explain, justify or substantiate.

To help focus on your emotions, complete one or more of the following sentences:

I was happy when …
I wish …
I get angry when I think of …
I'm afraid of …
I didn't like …
I feel sadness when …
I'm so angry that I feel like …
I miss …
I am relieved by …
Thank you because …
Thank you for letting me give/help you …
Sorry …
I wish that you …

As you write, you may experience that you immerse yourself so deeply into your own feelings that you forget time and place. Just let your tears flow. This can have a profound releasing effect.

Introductory and concluding greeting

Perhaps you would like to begin the letter with *dear*, *hello* or maybe *my dearest*? If it feels wrong no matter what you choose, skip the greeting to begin with and start with the letter itself.

You could conclude the letter with *love* or *hugs* or possibly just your name. How you feel about writing these greetings already says a lot about how you feel about your relationship with your relative.

The main points in Chapter 5: How to write a letter *to* your relative

- It may be advantageous to write the letter as a farewell letter.

- What you feel can be a basic feeling or a mixed feeling.

- You can identify your feelings with the help of your thoughts.

- Anger is often the upper layer. More vulnerable feelings can hide below, which can provide release if you can contact them.

- By saying thank you and sending good wishes, you let go of your bond to the person.

- Explanations often lead you astray.

- The opening and closing greeting of your letter reveals something about your feelings toward your relative.

CHAPTER 6

How to get the most out of it

Writing the letter is a big and important job. And you can get even more out of it if you also do some follow-up work. This chapter is about how you can increase your benefit of using ancestry therapy in different ways.

Fine-tune the letter

Set your letter aside for a few days, and then look at it again. If it moves you when you re-read it and you feel it's right to leave it in its original, authentic form, just skip the finishing touches. On the other hand, if you see that you have repeated yourself in different ways, you may want to shorten the letter to make it clearer. Or maybe you want to play with your sentences and try out new formulations. Perhaps you can find a new wording that is more precise and that releases or touches you in a deeper place.

Consider which parts of the letter move you the most and feel if the other parts are needed. One advantage of revising it is that it becomes nicer to read out loud, and you do not have to tire the reader with sections that you later see do not have much of an effect on you.

After a few days, when Amir re-read the letter he had written to himself from his mother, he discovered that his mother's long defensive speech had probably more to do with her needs than his. Like when he was a child, when he had been more in tune with her wishes than paying attention to his own. He chose to shorten all of his mother's excuses and instead allocate more space to what he wanted to hear: Her thanks for what he did for her while she was alive, her appreciation of him as a person and her recognition of the fight he fought.

While re-reading your letter, you can also consider whether you are satisfied with the opening greeting you chose and whether your closing feels right. Otherwise, you still have time to make it even more accurate, authentic or releasing.

The importance of reading the letter out loud

I would recommend that you initially read the letter out loud to yourself. As you listen to your own reading, you can feel if the letter is exactly as it should be. After that, it is a good idea to read it out to someone else. It is important that the person you choose is someone you feel comfortable with, so that you dare sense deep inside yourself while you are reading. It is best face to face, but it can also be done through an online meeting or on the phone.

You may be surprised how much more you sense your feelings when you share the letter, so do not cheat yourself of that experience. The better you sense your own emotional reaction to the letter, the deeper the new experience will be stored in your psyche and the more comprehensive your release will be.

If you don't know someone you want to ask, you can read it out to a tree in the forest, or you can book an appointment with a professional psychotherapist or psychologist. If you choose the latter, you also have someone to talk to about your letter process and the effect of the letter.

Time will uncover the benefits you gain from the letters

If you have been working on a relationship, for example with your mother, you may subsequently find that it has changed. This is a realisation that is likely to occur gradually over time. A few hours after you write the letter, you may begin to sense that something feels different. Two days later, the experience will probably begin to fall into place. After a few months or perhaps years, you may be somewhere new in relation to your mother, and you may want to try to write another letter or two.

Some people take a quantum leap in their personal development after working with ancestry therapy. For others, it will be one step, among many others, towards being better able to feel yourself and become who you are.

Should you show the letter to the other person?

If you have written a letter to yourself from a living relative, consider showing them the letter. If you are very brave, you can even ask if they will read it out to you.

In some cases, showing the letter to the person from whom it was written can open up a whole new conversation. Revealing what you long to hear can be an incredibly useful piece of information for your relative, who may never have fully understood how they can best make you happy.

However, there is the risk that the release you gained from the letter will fade if the person either says no or reads it out loud without putting the right feelings into it. There is also the risk that your relative perceives it as a criticism because she never expressed anything like what you wrote in the letter. She might feel that she is being pressured, that words are put in her mouth or that things are too personal.

If you have written a letter *to* your relative, you can also consider showing it. Many people are tempted to put all their cards on the table in this way. However, it pays to first consider how you think she will receive your letter. Will it make her open her heart, or will it make her close it? Also consider what you would like to get out of showing her the letter. And whether it is realistic.

In some relationships, showing the letters can open up a whole new level of honesty and a greater experience of closeness and interconnectedness. In other relationships, an honest letter can cause the other person to hide behind a shield. She might react in anger, or she might withdraw into herself and away from you because she cannot contain the pain or the guilt.

The risk of your letter creating distance is particularly great if it is written with anger as the driving force. But even if you have written the letter with love, it can make the recipient feel insecure. If she has never learned to express her positive feelings, she may feel that she owes you something that she is unable to give.

While considering whether to share your letter, the following exercise might be an eye-opener.

A letter to your ancestor as she would have written it

This exercise makes most sense if your relative is alive and if you want your relationship to improve. Imagine that she has been given the task you read about in the last chapter. She has to write a loving letter to herself from you. A letter that will give her a sense of release or just make her happy. What do you think she would write in the letter? Try to see if you can write it for her.

Afterwards, you can see if there is anything in the letter that you can accept responsibility for and make her happy about. She might be so touched by this that she softens up entirely and opens to you in a way that leads to a deeper and more loving relationship.

Be open that something new could happen

In Chapter Two, I described how Sarah's father, who knew nothing about the work Sarah had put into the letters, did something new when he unexpectedly took her hand. Time and again I hear that when one person in a relationship has worked extensively with that relationship – for example, using the tools in this book – the other person changes their behaviour. Even though they do not know anything about the work in question.

There is nothing particularly mysterious about this because when you have found peace in a relationship, you send out other non-verbal signals. For example, it may just be a micro-change in your tone of voice or in the expression on your face, which the other person picks up on and then starts acting a little differently towards you. This can easily happen without either of you consciously registering it. Suddenly there is just something new that is possible between you, and perhaps an old pattern of behaviour short-circuits itself and no longer works.

Just when Lena had decided how she would live with her relationship with her mother, her mother did something different. She surprised Lena by admitting that, for much of her life, she had focused a lot on her own problems, jobs and hobbies.

When Lena recovered a little from her mother's admission, which initially destroyed the peace she had found, she decided to reconsider whether the conversation she had opted out of having with her mother should now be given a second chance, or if she would want to see her mother a little more often.

Let more relatives onto your inner stage

The book is mostly about your relationship with your parents and grandparents. But you can easily invite more people. Maybe you knew one of your great-grandparents, or maybe you heard about them. It could also be a relative further back in the family that you know something about and feel an interest in.

For example, Sophie wrote a letter to her great-grandmother. Here is the beginning of the letter:

> *"Dear Marie,*
>
> *I have been told that you gave birth to 10 children, that your husband was sick and died while the youngest were still small, and that you then continued farming by yourself – with the help of your children. I believe you must be a strong woman. I would like to tell you something I have never said to anyone before ..."*

In the letter, Sophie spoke about her uncertainty concerning whether she was in the right relationship. Something she had not dared to talk to anyone else about. But since it was shared with great-grandmother Marie, it no longer felt so dangerous.

When months or years have passed after you have written your letters, you may find that a new situation in your life calls for a letter from a new relative. And if you have first established contact, for example by using letters, you can return to them whenever you want or need to.

Maintain the connection to your relative

If you have had a good exchange of letters with a deceased relative, you may enjoy continuing to talk to them about your life. Forty-seven-year-old Karen explains:

> *I was in my late twenties when my grandmother died, and the older I get, the more I learn how much I resemble her. It makes me feel good to look at a picture of her and tell her about my life. Especially on days when I have my head filled with worries or am deeply in doubt about something. I know she understands.*
>
> *While I entrust her with everything, I often cry, and afterwards I feel comforted and redeemed. And the advantage of talking to her rather than, say, a friend is that I dare to be more honest since I have nothing to lose. Furthermore, I do not have to hear about her life afterwards, which in some situations I hardly have the energy for.*

Karen has a picture of her grandmother in a drawer. She takes it out when she needs to share great joy as well as when she needs to lighten her heart and cry.

Use ancestry therapy in other relationships

Several people have asked me if they can use the method in relation to a brother or a sister. The answer is yes. For example, you can also use it in relation to a stepparent, teacher, partner or friend. As a client exclaimed: "It's a great way to get some things done in relation to your family or others."

The main points in Chapter 6: How to benefit the most

- Fine-tuning your letter can make it stronger.
- If you read the letter out loud to someone else, it will probably increase the intensity of your feelings.
- Your benefit from the letters will become apparent over time.
- Showing the letter to the person to whom it is written can sometimes be fruitful, while at other times it can increase the distance between you.
- You may find that your relative changes their behaviour despite not knowing anything about the letters.
- Some people benefit from continuing the exchange with one or more relatives.
- You can also use ancestry therapy in other relationships.

CHAPTER 7
If your relative burdens you

There may be challenges in using ancestry therapy in relation to a relative who is still alive. Especially if she is a burden to you in one way or another. It can be difficult to find peace with a relationship if something continues to happen which makes you sad or you feel pressured. Perhaps everyone can see the way she is burdening you, or perhaps you just feel bad when you are with her without really knowing why.

Consider taking a break from seeing each other

While working with a relationship, for example with your mother, being in contact with her can be disruptive. After all, the letter should be from her as she is in her essence, without the disruptive veil of counterproductive self-protection. If she calls in the middle of your letter process and imposes her own needs upon you, it can be difficult to maintain the image.

Perhaps you can tell her before you start that you need to take a break from each other and cut contact for a few days or weeks. You can probably find a loving white lie to justify it if the truth does not feel right to say.

For example, a client said that her therapist had asked her to hold a silent retreat at home in her spare time for a while to immerse herself in her personal work with herself and reduce stress. Her mother could call her boyfriend if there was something important.

Do not overdo seeing your relative in her essence

You're not meant to relate permanently to your living ancestor as she is in her essence instead of dealing with her as the person you see. You can see her in her essence as an experiment while writing the letter to yourself. And you may find that the result is that she actually becomes more loving toward you. As mentioned above, sometimes when one person has worked meticulously with the relationship, the other changes their behaviour. Even if she knows nothing about the work.

However, we must otherwise be realistic. Your letters might not have that effect. Perhaps she is not in contact with her essence and feels that the way you see her is not right. And if she treats you badly and you continue to write loving letters to yourself from her, you might not be taking precautions and taking care of yourself.

Is your relative violent?

If you experience physical violence from your relative, it is important that you establish a boundary and stop the violence. I would advise you not to write to yourself from her before your boundary is set and respected. In this case, it is not about contacting the soft and vulnerable feelings; instead, it is about having the courage to set a boundary.

This also applies if you are a victim of psychological violence. If you are in doubt about what psychological violence can be, you can see some examples below.

Casting suspicion
Disproportionate accusations
Criticism of the person you are
Personal attacks
Scornful remarks
Negative comparisons – for example, with siblings
Scold in an unloving way
Hateful looks
Rolls her eyes when you say something
Threats

If one of your relatives behaves violently, it is important that you say stop clearly and unambiguously. You can write a letter to her expressing all your feelings and enjoying the relief it can give. But it is even more important to clearly say no.

Maja did this by writing the following to her father:

> *"Dear Dad,*
>
> *I am happy with your advice regarding everything practical about my home and my things. But, with respect to who I am as a person and the way I have lived or live my life, I will not listen to any more good tips,*

criticism or assessments in the future. Should I need your advice in personal matters, I will ask myself.

I want you to respect this – otherwise, you have to be prepared that I will hang up or walk away.

Love, Maja"

As an adult, you do not need to put up with scolding or negative judgements of the person you are. And the clearer you are when you say no and the more consistently you enforce your limit, the more likely it is that the violence will stop.

Don't let your relative burden you

If you feel bad when you spend time with your relative or afterwards, without there being any violence, you can use ancestry therapy to determine the reason. By writing to yourself from her, you can examine what wishes and needs you have at stake in the relationship. And by writing to her, you can practice expressing what you feel in relation to her. Afterwards, you may have the courage to talk to her about it.

If you cannot find the courage to have the conversation, if the conversation does not work as intended or if you are just too unsure about what is going on between you, it may be a good idea to seek help. If possible, you can visit a therapist together, who can help you understand the emotions each of you is struggling with. Couples therapy is not just for couples; it can also be used by others, for example, a father and a son. It is important that the therapist is trained and experienced in couples therapy. This will enable her to make sure that the conversation proceeds slowly enough so there is time to check that everyone is OK and to change track if the conversation is about to die or hit a dead end. A couples therapist will also provide tools for changing the way you interact together.

If you have tried to talk to your relative about it without getting anywhere, and if professional help does not work, you can protect yourself by limiting the time you spend with the relative in question.

Parents or grandparents should not burden their children or grandchildren to such an extent that they have less to pass on.

You may not be able to see exactly what it is that affects you negatively. But it doesn't have to prevent you from writing or saying, as honestly and concretely as possible, something like:

"Mum, I can't explain why, but I feel bad from being together with you. That is something I have been struggling with for many years. It's so bad that I sometimes go home and throw up. It's important to me that we stay connected, but if you sometimes find me dismissive, you know why.

It's not something we can change, Mum, it's just how it is. It is not because there is anything wrong with either you or me. And I don't want you to put pressure on me. I will tell you when I want us to meet and for how long."

To say something like that can be a huge relief. But being that honest can be scary. To my mother, I chose instead to make excuses with small white lies. I did not dare do anything else. But it came at a high price. In my attempt to avoid hurting my mother, I ended up burdening myself instead. The result was that I alone had to bear all the blame for the short visits and the shame that I was looking forward to her dying. Today I would probably have chosen differently.

Another way of saying no to a burdensome relative may be this:

"Mum, I am very grateful for the life you have given me. And in order to protect it and to pass it on in the best possible way, I need to limit contact with you so that I do not spend too much effort on something that is extinguishing the light in my eyes."

This formulation is probably less suitable to use on a parent. But it can be a good way for you to think about your choice to limit contact. In other words, that out of respect for your place among your kin and for what you have received and what you have to pass on, you choose to limit contact.

Parents must not burden their children with guilt or shame. Not even if the children have grown up. Someone needs to stop it. If parents lack the self-insight and wisdom to do so, the adult child has to find the courage to say what could be perceived as hurtful. Otherwise, it can easily end up that the price for the lack of boundaries is paid by your children, who sense that you are under pressure and drained of energy, and they may consciously or subconsciously blame themselves.

The main points in Chapter 7: If your relative is burdening you

- The idea is not that you should permanently relate to your living relative as she is in her essence. Perhaps you should not be in contact while you work with ancestry therapy.
- Do not let your relative burden you with guilt and shame.
- If physical or psychological violence exists between you, it is important to stop the violence first. After that, you can use ancestry therapy.

CHAPTER 8
Alternative exercises

Here are some exercises you can use if you do not like writing or if you want to switch between writing letters and other effective tools. Here you will use the same instructions and inspiration lists as when writing letters. Just replace the written word with speech, as I will demonstrate in this chapter.

Here, too, you first need to choose which relative to start with. Then, when you are ready, create a peaceful and quiet environment and give yourself plenty of time. Once you have done that, feel inside yourself and connect with the feelings, the loss or the longing you sense when you imagine the person sitting or facing you.

Use dolls

At the back of the book, you will find a sheet of folding paper dolls that you can cut out and use.

Choose one of the dolls to be the person in the relationship you want to work with. And choose another doll to be you.

Place the dolls on the table in front of you and check to make sure the distance between them is appropriate. Perhaps one would prefer to stand sideways or facing away. Move them around a little until it feels right for you.

Prepare to speak on behalf of one of the dolls. Let us say you chose your grandfather. Imagine he is present in his essence and let him say something to you that you would be happy to hear. Gently touch him with your finger as he speaks.

As with letter writing, you can also choose to be the one who begins. Perhaps you have feelings you need to express before communication can come to life the other way. In this case, take the opportunity to express all the sorrow, fear, joy, gratitude or anger you feel toward him.

Once you have spoken out, you may be ready to let the other doll say something, but you might also need a few days to pass so that the experience of what you have said can settle into your system before taking the next step.

Instead of dolls, you can also collect stones on the beach and use them. The stones should preferably be roughly equal in size. It is not "the big one" talking to "the little one", but rather an adult talking to the adult person you are today. Just as it is the person you are right now talking to the other person.

In the same way as it is important that you read the written letter, it is also important that you re-hear what you have said. You can record it on your phone. You could benefit from listening to your recording again after a few days, when you might get even more out of hearing it. And if you know someone who wants to listen with you, you will gain even more.

Say it out loud to a picture

Another option is to say what is in your heart to a picture of the person in the relationship you are working on. And if you talk to yourself from the perspective of your relative, you could talk to a picture of yourself, ideally a recent one.

It is important that you say it out loud and not just think what you want to say inside your head. Here, too, you should remember to record your speech. Having it on paper or in an audio file will lead to far greater clarity. When you revisit it later, it will be easier to see things from a somewhat external perspective, and something entirely new could happen.

Imagine your relative on a chair in front of you

A third option is to set up two chairs opposite each other. Imagine your relative in one chair, then sit in the other chair. Once you have sat down, you can begin by inhaling and exhaling deeply a few times and feel that the chair is carrying you. If you have chosen to start as yourself, imagine your relative on the opposite chair. What is she wearing? What is her posture like, and how is her facial expression?

Feel what sitting opposite her does to you. Does the distance between you feel right, or should one of the chairs be moved?

Do you feel relaxed or tense? Does it stir up feelings? Or does it give you inspiration to say something to the person?

Feel inward and say whatever comes to mind to the person you are imagining in the empty chair.

When you have nothing more to say, you can move to the other chair. This is just like writing to yourself from your relative. Here you should try to be your relative as she is in her essence, where she is unspoiled by the mental scratches and scars that life has given her. As your relative, you should say the positive things you have to give. For example, you can start with: "I am your mother, Karen." Then you could continue like this: "Now I want to tell you what I love most about you … " Or: "I am sorry about the times when I overlooked you and your good intentions; for example, when you …"

When you are in your relative's shoes and have no more to say, sit in your own chair and sense how it feels to receive what you just heard. Was it nice? Were you touched? Or is there something missing?

You can switch back and forth between the chairs several times and let a dialogue take place. Here, too, you must remember to record it and listen to it afterwards and feel its effect on you.

Someone working within psychiatry recounted how, from time to time, one of the clients he visits does not want to see him again and does not want to say goodbye. Instead, the client just contacts his manager and asks for a new social worker. However, this leaves him with a need to bring closure to the relationship he has with the client in a good way. Especially when it comes to one of the clients he has visited for several years. Here he often uses the chair method and finds peace that way. For him, it works well if he starts by scolding the client: "Who do you think you are?" But every time he switches chairs, the tone grows milder. When he later remembers the client, he remembers the conversations he had in the chairs rather than a sense of rejection or the anger it caused.

Similarly, your letter, speech or chair work may be what you associate with your relative in the future. And it can be a particularly profound sense of relief if you had negative thoughts or memories associated with that person.

The main points in Chapter 8: Alternative exercises

- Instead of using letters, you can choose to say what you would have written to a picture or to a paper doll.
- You can also let a dialogue take place between two chairs that you set up opposite each other. Your relative speaks from one, and you speak from the other.

CHAPTER 9

Forgiveness

If your relationship with a relative is difficult or ambivalent, you might wonder if you need to forgive her. Over the years, there have been many different perceptions of what it means to forgive. Some believe forgiveness only occurs when you are no longer angry or when you come to an acceptance of what the other person did. But by this definition, forgiveness is often not possible.

Forgiveness is giving something to the offender

I find the explanation offered by priest and psychotherapist Bent Falk to be very useful. According to him, as the Word says, to forgive is to "give", and to this we can add "despite". To forgive is a decision you can choose to make. It is not about no longer feeling angry, nor is it about feeling love for the other person. You do not have control over your feelings anyway. Feelings are as they are until they change and become something else. You can forgive even if you still feel the pain or get angry every time you think of what happened; for example, if you suffered verbal abuse or were let down.

Here are three examples of what forgiveness may look like:

- I wish you had taken better care of me when I was a child, but it was as it was. I think you did your best, so now I will try to move on and focus on the positive experiences we had and have together.

- Although I can still get angry when I think of what you did, I will try not to be unnecessarily negative. And I will remind myself that your intentions were good, that every person has her struggles and that I do not know yours.

- I still don't think that what you did is acceptable, but now I think I've scolded you enough about it, so from now on I'll focus on what I learned from it and on the good experiences we've had together.

Bent Falk once said that when people say sorry, what they really mean is do not punish me. I think it is well spotted.

Some people do not think they have forgiven enough or in the right way. To investigate it further, I often ask: "If the offender admitted that what she did was not good and pleaded with you not to punish her for it, what would you answer?" Often the respondent answers quickly and with a pure heart: "Of course I won't punish her." Then my answer is: Then *you have* forgiven.

Negative emotions and self-protection

Even if you have forgiven, you may still have many different negative and positive emotions in relation to the person in question. And you may find that when you are in a room with the person, your self-protection strategies begin to activate, preventing you from being fully present and putting you on your guard. The other may experience your distance as a punishment. But that is probably not the intention. It might just take some time before you feel completely comfortable again. Or maybe your self-protection strategies have started automatically and are beyond your control.

Sometimes your defences are smarter than you. Perhaps your head has not yet understood what your instincts and your body already know, namely that there may be something in the relationship that you should be protecting yourself from. For example, your relative may basically not have the strength to live up to the improvement she promised you. Or that her own trauma, needs or problems in life strain her to the extent that she does not have the energy to see you on your terms.

Another reason why your relationship continues to be distant, even if you try to forgive, may be that you do not want to face reality. Some of the ways we keep up our guard towards one another are because of this. As long as you are concerned with keeping someone at a distance, you can avoid feeling your own helplessness, pain or sorrow. Or put another way: Your anger can be a defence against feeling your own vulnerability.

Face your loss and let go

When we find it difficult to forgive, it is often because we find it difficult to let go of a hope of getting some kind of compensation. That hope may be more or less subconscious. You may not even realise how unwilling you are to accept the damage and loss you have suffered. Even if you know somewhere deep down that what happened cannot be undone, there may well be another part of you that refuses to face that fact.

Let us say a traffic accident left you lame. As long as you are preoccupied with being angry with the driver and with reprimanding him and filing complaints, you are focused on the past. And it protects you from dealing with your new situation. The day you are ready to accommodate your own emotional reaction to your loss, you will be able to let go of the past and forgive the driver.

You could also be in a situation where you were left with psychological scars after neglect or a trauma in your childhood. Here the mechanism is the same, but it is much more difficult to be paid damages, so it really pays to let go of the past and instead face your losses, weep and move on.

You may subconsciously fear that if you accept the loss, you will feel a sorrow so overwhelming that it is hard to contain. A lot of mental rigidity is basically a fear of falling apart. If you are unsure whether you can endure the emotions that will force themselves on you if you let go of your fight with the person who hurt you, you should train the ability to contain emotions. You can read about this in the next chapter. And then it will be a matter of time before you grow strong enough to be with your own emotional response to your past.

The main points in Chapter 9: Forgiveness

- Forgiveness means giving something to the offender.
- This does not mean that you should no longer have negative feelings.
- You may still need to protect yourself.
- If you find it difficult to forgive, it may be because you are afraid of not being able to accommodate your own emotional reaction to face your loss and let go of hope for compensation.

CHAPTER 10

Meet your feelings with open curiosity

When you write letters, talk to a picture, or otherwise work with ancestry therapy, new feelings may appear that you feel uncomfortable with. Or familiar feelings may appear with a new intensity. You might want to escape from the situation and put the work on the shelf. But that would be a shame because, when feelings you do not often feel or which are not normally this intense step onto your stage, you have the opportunity to learn something new. Had Sarah from Chapter Two failed to take her letter out of her bag and read it out loud, she would have missed an experience that was deeply releasing.

In this chapter, you will get different advice and tools that can help you be with the emotions you feel without fleeing or panicking.

Care about your feelings

If, for example, you do not like yourself when you are angry, you can train to adopt a new attitude. See yourself with your mind's eye as you are when you are angry. Write a loving letter to the person you see or talk to her lovingly, for example, through a paper doll.

I could say or write to myself:

> *"Dear Angry Ilse,*
>
> *That's quite a force that dwells in you. You find it difficult to contain it. That's fine. You will learn. It's good that you are practicing. Emotions cannot be either good or evil. They simply exist. They show up even when they are not invited. Your feelings cannot be your fault.*
>
> *It is OK to be angry. You are always allowed to feel the way you feel.*
>
> *Love from your best friend"*

You can also directly address the feeling you feel right now, which can sometimes have an even more profound effect. For example, write or say:

> *"Dear Grief,*
>
> *It's OK that you are there. I will meet you with open curiosity. I will refrain from trying to change you. Instead, I will listen to you and let you be entirely as you are. You can be here with all your weight. The two of us will be good friends.*
>
> *Love, Ilse"*

When you want to find your inner peace, the trick is to say yes to what is, instead of trying to bring yourself somewhere else. Naturally, there is nothing wrong with going for a walk, seeking company or physical exercise to improve your mood. There is no need to cultivate sadness, for example. But if you never dare to look your sadness in the eyes or feel it in your body, you risk living with a distance to your inner self.

Many of us only like a part of what we feel inside. And then we spend a lot of energy trying to escape from the rest. Doubt is an example of a condition that most people want to get away from. For example, if you are in doubt about whether you should keep or leave your job, you would of course like to figure it out. But try also saying yes to the doubt. It is OK to be in doubt. It is always OK to feel the way you feel. With doubt, several options are open. And if you can find peace in being with the doubt as if it were a friend, the right direction will present itself when the time comes.

The same goes for any feeling or condition. If you are able to welcome what you feel without trying to fight it, it will probably affect your inner self for a while, and then it will wane and let itself be replaced by a new inner experience.

The sense of calm you get from having the ability to contain yourself

Being able to contain yourself means being able to accept your own inner self and all the diversity of life you carry within. Acceptance here is not to be understood as a brain matter. It is not enough that your mind approves what you feel. For example, you can accept your anger with your head and think it is reasonable, and at the same time you can find it difficult to tolerate feeling the anger in your body. And you may think that love is a beautiful feeling and yet have anxiety symptoms such as unease, palpitations or dizziness when it grows strong.

You contain a feeling when you open yourself to it with your whole being and can endure feeling it in your body and being with it without escaping.

A lot of tension and anxiety are really about feelings you find difficult to contain. If you are good at containing yourself, you can better relax and give yourself time to listen to your inner self and find out what you need to do, even when your feelings are raging.

When you fall short containing a feeling

For example, you might want to take responsibility for your feelings and yet still find that when your anger intensifies, you lose self-control. This is certainly something most people can relate to. The same applies to the situation where you end up letting your anger loose on someone, even if that was not what you wanted deep down. You may experience it as if your body does not have sufficient inner space to contain the feeling, which instead seeps out as sharp remarks, condescending body language or slander. Or it crashes like a giant wave out through your mouth, as if you vomited on someone.

When you cannot stand being with the feeling that currently dominates your inner stage, you can easily end up acting too quickly. You might crumple the letter or the paper dolls and throw them away and give up on learning the method.

Why you may have a hard time containing a feeling

The ability to contain your own feelings is largely inherited through the generations. You probably feel comfortable with the feelings with which your parents had a relaxed relationship. At the same time, there may be other feelings that your parents and grandparents could hardly bear to feel. And which you therefore never received support to be at peace with.

In some families, you can feel and express yourself safely. In other families, showing a certain feeling can result in being ignored or reprimanded. Your own ability to be with your feelings is strongly influenced by how easy or difficult it was for your parents to contain their own feelings and thus yours.

Sally is an example of a parent who finds it difficult to contain her own feelings and therefore cannot contain her child's. When Sally's boy falls down, she shouts: "Up again!" almost before he hits the ground. He gets no time or help to exist with the feeling, and the boy learns that you should not feel what hurts. He may later find it difficult to help his own children to contain their pain.

Another example may be Marie, who turns away from her son when he is angry. Perhaps her son's anger reminds her of unpleasant experiences she has had with her father. In any case, she feels agitation or displeasure when he is angry and therefore finds it difficult to maintain eye contact with him. The boy is thus left alone with his anger and will probably try to deal with it using unhealthy strategies, such as displacing it or acting it out in an inappropriate way that leads to conflict with his surroundings.

An example of a parent who helps his child contain a feeling is Rasmus. When his daughter falls, he holds her until she has finished crying. He may also help her find the words for her feeling. He might say: "Ow, ow, this hurts."

Sophie is another example. When her daughter shows anger, she mirrors the anger with mimicry and body language and says: "You are angry, little friend. That's fine." And the child experiences that her mother can contain her anger. This way, she gets to know her anger and practices containing it herself.

Some parents manage to create a space where everything that is felt can be expressed without making it seem wrong. They teach their child to find peace, even when the child is experiencing waves of emotions on the inside. And the child gradually develops a relaxed relationship with his or her own **emotions, thoughts and desires.** Other parents can contain some of the children's feelings, but perhaps there is one that they find too difficult and therefore ignore.

If your parents ignored or reacted negatively to one of your feelings, you will probably find it difficult to contain and love that feeling today. You may experience having difficulty being in your own body when it is activated. For one family, anger is a feeling that may not be expressed. For another, it is sorrow or fear, which they see as a sign of weakness. And in yet another, joy may be regarded as noisy or just as a painful reminder of what some members of the family are missing.

Many parents do not know that it is important to teach children to contain their feelings. My parents did not know. When I was most excited, my father yelled angrily: "Turn it down!" No wonder that, for me, powerful joy was associated with anxiety.

I think my grandfather shouted the same thing at my father. And my great-grandfather, who was sick, may have yelled it even louder. Difficulty in containing a certain feeling has often been passed down over several generations and is in fact no one's fault. But you have the opportunity to stop the negative legacy and pass on something better.

A greater capacity to contain improves your freedom of action

When we experience discomfort while being in the same room as someone else, most of us think that the other person is the cause. In a way, this is true because the other person awakens feelings in us that we have a hard time with. We can solve it by avoiding the other person, but there is a better option, namely that you work on being better at containing and loving all your own feelings.

There may still be good reasons to avoid a relationship; for example, if the other person is treating you badly. But if her mere presence makes you uncomfortable, it is wise to take a closer look at what she awakens in you. Maybe it is a feeling that you can come to love.

The better you become at loving all the diversity of the life you have inside, the more freedom you will have. And the less likely you will be to act too quickly on your feelings or to avoid people or situations.

A good capacity to contain will also make you more resilient to relational pain and stress and therefore give you the courage to go deeper into your relationships. It will also make you more resilient to anxiety, as much anxiety is rooted in displaced emotions. If you dare welcome all your feelings and acknowledge each one, you will be on very solid ground.

How to increase your capacity to contain

I, too, have been afraid of my feelings. Afraid that they would grow big and blow me up from the inside or wash me away so I would never again be able to find a foothold. For example, when I feel sad, I still get a strong urge to check social media. If I give in to the urge, half an hour may suddenly have passed, and I will have distanced myself greatly from being able to feel myself.

If, instead, I pull myself together and sit on my meditation pillow – even though it is the last thing I feel like doing – things get better. I close my eyes and inhale and exhale deeply a few times. I let the inhaled air push my body to expand in the front, back and sides. I ask the universe to help me open up and welcome the thing that is pressuring me. And I remind myself that I am greater than my feelings. Then I surrender myself to be with what is. Maybe my feelings trigger sobbing, which I let elapse like a passing rain. Once I have experienced the feeling for a while, it dampens, and I can continue doing whatever I was doing.

Another example may be when I wake up at night with a sense of despair and desperation, while my brain is busy looking for a way out that does not seem to exist. The strategy that I automatically start with is to try to find a solution. But, if instead of engaging with my stressed thoughts I pay attention to my body, things improve. Then I lie for a while and pay attention to my breathing. I follow how the air rushes in through my nostrils, makes my chest and stomach rise, then flows out again. I open myself to feel the despair. It is part of life. It is allowed to be here. If I stop fighting against feeling what I feel, I often experience warmth flowing throughout my body. A warmth that calms me down.

I am not always that thorough. Sometimes I just stop for a few seconds, take a deep breath and feel my body all the way into my fingers and toes and remain curious to whatever is pressuring me. A feeling that is welcomed and receives attention often fades out on its own.

If you are overwhelmed by a feeling, you should try to stay with it, even if you probably want to escape from the situation through thoughts or actions.

There are times when you cannot give yourself the proper care at that moment. Maybe you are in a meeting and get so annoyed with your manager that you are about to flip out. In such cases, wait until you are in a quiet environment before practicing how to contain yourself.

When circumstances are suitable for contemplation, you can slowly go through the situation in your mind and hope the feeling reappears so that you can direct your curiosity toward it. Here, it is not important to find the root of your reaction. Ideally, you should not look for a cause, analyse or speculate. Accept that the feeling is there and experience it with your senses. Where in your body do you feel it? Do you get cold or hot? What quality does its energy have? Is there a quiver, bubbling or perhaps a tremor? Does it have a colour, a smell, a taste or a sound? Be curious about how it can be felt in different parts of the body. Does your face want to grimace? Do your hands want to open or close?

Instead of contracting in fear, try to expand so that you have room for the feeling in your body. Inhale and exhale deeply a few times. Every second you manage to be together with the feeling without stiffening and without acting, you have become a little more accustomed to it and expanded your capacity to contain. It is like putting on a pair of freshly washed jeans that feel tight. If you stay in them, they expand and become more pleasant to wear.

Every time you feel an urge to avoid someone or something, you may ask yourself: Could I instead use this opportunity to practice how to contain my feelings? You can train your ability to contain yourself like you can train a muscle. If you do not lift anything heavy, you get thin arms. And if you always choose to withdraw physically or mentally in the face of difficult emotions, you will be fragile when you experience them. But if you challenge yourself, your capacity to contain grows with the task.

Instead of escaping from a feeling that is more intense than you are used to, it is important to stay in it and be curious about your inner reaction. However, only to a point. If your feeling is so strong that you forget to breathe and do not feel your body and thus remain grounded, the challenge is too great. The same applies if you find that you disappear from the situation in your thoughts. Consider taking a hot bath or have a foot bath. It will strengthen your contact with your body and make the situation easier for you. You can also take a break and be physically active, for example, by taking a walk.

Share your feeling with someone else

If you find that there is a certain feeling where, time and again, you fall short or a particular situation that is difficult to be in, consider asking someone else to help you. Two people together can contain more than one. If you have difficulty with a feeling or a pain, it can help you to have body contact or eye contact with someone else while you feel it. If eye contact is to be healing, it requires that the owner of the other pair of eyes has a relaxed relationship with that feeling. It can be a caring friend, a psychotherapist or a psychologist.

When you talk about the feeling, avoid justifications. You do not need that. Quite the contrary, justifying your feeling will lead you astray and make it harder for you to feel it. As mentioned earlier, explanations are unnecessary. It is OK to have feelings that you cannot explain. You are always allowed to feel the way you feel. Actions may be wrong, but your feelings and sensations are as they are – whether you like them or not.

Instead of: "I am furious because …", you will get greater release by expressing what you sense, for example: "I am furious, and I can feel it in my body like this:

- My whole body is trembling.
- I can't find peace.
- I'm ice cold inside.
- My muscles are tensing up.
- I am sweating.
- My arms are quivering."

When you feel your body, you will be more grounded and more in the present. It is precisely this anchoring in the body that will help you to contain your feeling.

You are more than your thoughts and feelings

Feelings and other states of being come and go. Throughout your life, many different thoughts and feelings have appeared in your consciousness and disappeared again. You are the one who experiences the many different ways of feeling. And, at your core, you are the same as you were when you first looked out through your eyes as a newborn. Later you looked through child eyes, teenage eyes, and then through the adult eyes you are looking through today.

You can see your inner experiences as clouds floating by. You are the heaven, which is far more constant than an emotion, thought or sensation that drifts past.

When I meet a feeling that I try to contain, I remind myself that I am more than my feelings or thoughts. I am the one who experiences them. And the more I identify with being the one who is witness to my emotions, rather than identifying with the feeling itself, the more grounded I feel.

Grief is a natural part of a self-development process

If you have used the tools in this book sufficiently in-depth and have gained new, life-enhancing insight, you may have come into contact with both relief and sorrow. Relief is one of the great pleasures of life. Grief is often a sign of health. When something has become less difficult, you have the capacity to feel how hard it was before this point.

Many people ask themselves: "Why didn't I discover this a long time ago?" This is a good question that can provide new insights. Ask with curiosity and with a light tone, but make sure you do not ponder on it for so long that you are weighed down by self-reproach. If you ask and do not receive an answer, just drop it. You can easily do without the knowledge that lies in the answer.

If you have focused on the reason why you did not get the new insight sooner, you should also remember to direct the light of consciousness toward your resources. For example, you can do this by asking: "What qualities led me to gaining this insight now?" Perhaps it was your courage, your willpower, your intuition or your perseverance that brought you to the place where the new knowledge could manifest itself.

The grief associated with feeling how hard your life has been is a good process that heals. Allow yourself to be particularly vulnerable for a period of time and be extra caring towards yourself. When grief fades, you are likely to feel stronger and more robust in the face of life's challenges.

The main points in Chapter 10: Meet your feelings with open curiosity

- The better you can accommodate and care for your feelings, the easier you can find your inner peace, and the greater your freedom of action.
- Your capacity to contain is to some degree inherited from your ancestry.

- You can train your capacity to contain just like you train a muscle.
- Having eye contact with someone else when starting to experience a feeling can help you contain it.
- When you share your feeling, it's good to focus on how the feeling is felt in the body.
- Grief is often a good process and a sign of health.
- You are more than your thoughts and feelings.

Peace work is spreading

Many of us wait for years for someone else to change. I remember writing angry letters to my father when I was very young, hoping that he would realise that he had to behave differently. Later it was my boyfriends I tried to change. All with very little success.

When you embark on ancestry therapy, you are creating a change in yourself. And it will infect your loved ones and inspire them to seek peace for themselves. This way, your work can extend far beyond you. The peace you create will spread like ripples in the water and will be transmitted to future generations.

If everyone would be careful to foster peace – both inside and around them – conflicts could be resolved more quickly, and wars could be avoided.

I hope you found inspiration in the book to find peace with your ancestors so that you can open yourself to them as a funnel and receive their blessing and the good things they have to give you.

With the support of your ancestry, you can feel free to be who you are, so you can be a good example and can afford to be generous with yourself and what you pass on.

Good luck,
Ilse Sand

ACKNOWLEDGMENTS

I wish to thank the following:

Registered psychotherapist and master of theology Bent Falk, who himself is the author of several books, including the bestseller *Honest Dialogue*. Bent Falk has been invaluable to me, both in my personal and professional development.

MSC in psychology and, until his death, head of the Institute for Gestalt Analysis, Niels Hoffmeyer. He was a source of great inspiration to me for many years.

Thanks, too, to all of you who have read the book and given me feedback: Margith Christiansen, Lene Broe Dahl, Christine Grøntved, Martin Håstrup, Jan Kaa Kristensen, Ulla Larsen, Jørn Blander Nielsen, Kirstine Sand, Jørgen Schmidt and Lone Søgaard. Each of you has put your mark on this book.

LITERATURE FOR INSPIRATION

Buber, Martin: *I and Thou*. Martino Fine Books, 2010.

Davidsen-Nielsen, Marianne, and Nini Leick: *Healing Pain: Attachment, Loss, and Grief Therapy*. Routledge, 1991.

Della Selva, Patricia Coughlin: *Intensive Short-Term Dynamic Psychotherapy: Theory and Technique*. London: Karnac Books, 1996.

Falk, Bent: *Honest Dialogue. Presence, Common Sense, and Boundaries When You Want to Help Someone*. Jessica Kingsley Publishers, 2017.

Fischer, Doris Elisabeth: *Unravel Entanglements With Love*. Familieopstiller, 2018.

Hart, S.: *Brain, Attachment, Personality: An Introduction to Neuroaffective Development*. Routledge, 2008.

Jung, C. G.: *The Undiscovered Self*. Berkley. 2006.

Kierkegaard, Søren: *The Sickness unto Death*. Penguin Classics; First Printing edition, August 1, 1989.

Kierkegaard, Søren: *The Concept of Anxiety*. Princeton University Press; First Edition (US) First Printing edition, February 1, 1981.

Miller, Alice: *The Drama of the Gifted Child*. Basic Books, 1997.

O'Toole, Donna: *Aarvy Aardvark Finds Hope*. Compassion Press, 1988.

Sand, Ilse: *Confronting Shame: How to Understand Your Shame and Gain Inner Freedom*. Jessica Kingsley Publishers, 2022.

Sand, Ilse: *Come Closer*. Jessica Kingsley Publishers, 2017.

Sand, Ilse: *Highly Sensitive People in an Insensitive World: How to Create a Happy Life*. Jessica Kingsley Publishers, 2016.

Sand, Ilse: *On Being an Introvert or Highly Sensitive Person – a Guide to Boundaries, Joy, and Meaning*. Jessica Kingsley Publishers, 2018.

Sand, Ilse: *See Yourself with Friendly Eyes – How to Let Go of Guilt*. Ammentorp, 2023.

Sand, Ilse: *The Emotional Compass: How to Think Better About Your Feelings*. Jessica Kingsley Publishers, 2016.

Sand, Ilse: *Helping Through Conversation: Specific Advice, Ideas and Instructions*. Ammentorp, 2023.

Tolle, Eckhart: *The Power of Now: A Guide to Spiritual Enlightenment.* New World Library, 2010.

Yalom, Irvin D.: *Existential Psychotherapy.* Basic Books, 1980.

BY THE SAME AUTHOR

See Yourself with Friendly Eyes:
How to Let Go of Guilt
Tools to help you let go of an exaggerated guilty conscience
and train to look at yourself with friendly eyes.

Confronting Shame:
How to Understand Your Shame and Gain Inner
Freedom
A book about letting go of the fear that
something is wrong with you.
How you can understand your shame and the
problems it causes.

Come Closer – On Love and Self-Protection
On how unconscious self-protection strategies can get in
the way of vibrant, loving connections, and how these
strategies can be fought by making them conscious.

The Emotional Compass: How to Think Better About
Your Feelings
On what feelings can mean and how to get in touch with
them.

**Highly Sensitive People in an Insensitive World:
How to Create a Happy Life**
On highly sensitive people and shame, guilt, and
communication.

Helping Through Conversation
Specific advice, ideas and instructions

on how to use psychotherapeutic tools in supportive
dialogues,

and how to take care of yourself as a helper.

On Being an Introvert or Highly Sensitive Person
– a Guide to Boundaries, Joy and Meaning
What does it mean to be an introvert or highly sensitive?
And what is the difference?
Good advice and tools for handling different situations
with which introverts and highly sensitive people often
have difficulty.

Read more at ilsesand.com

ANNEX

Folding paper dolls A

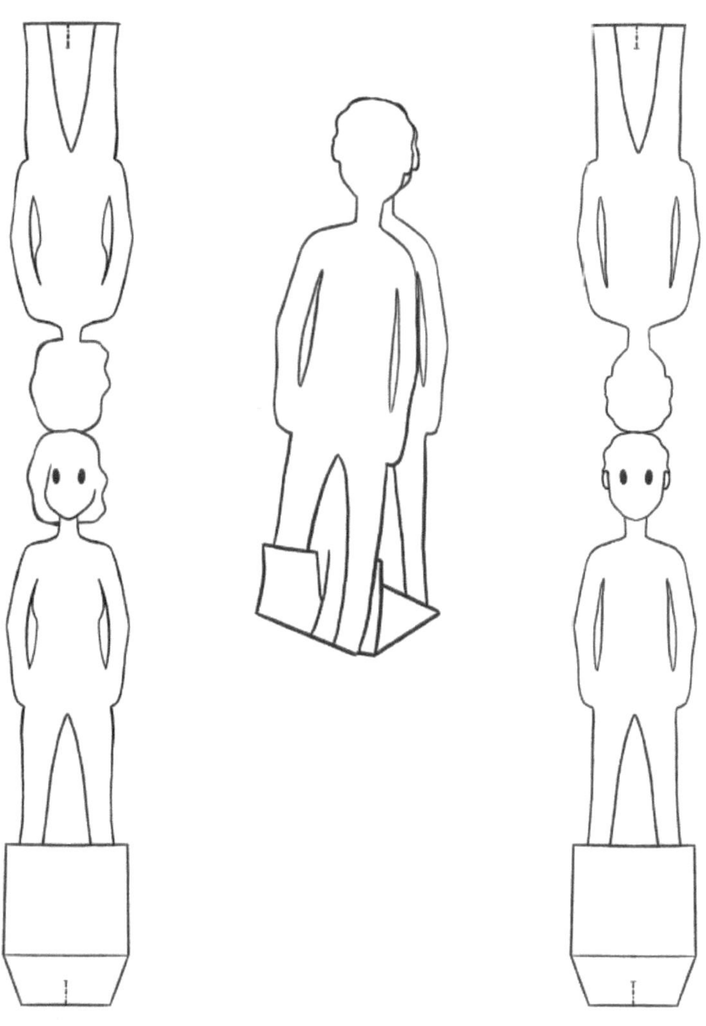

Folding paper dolls B

9 788879 268335 9